A CONCISE GUIDE TO
HORSES &
PONIES

A CONCISE GUIDE TO
HORSES &
PONIES

Corinne Clark

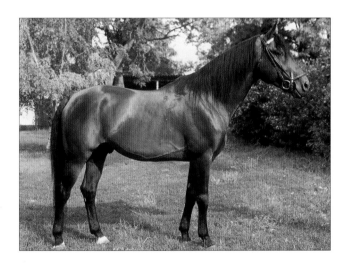

Bath · New York · Singapore · Hong Kong · Cologne · Delhi · Melbourne

This is a Parragon Book
First published in 2007

Parragon Books Ltd
Queen Street House
4 Queen Street
Bath, BA1 1HE

Produced by Atlantic Publishing

See page 256 for
photograph copyright details
Text © Parragon Books Ltd 2007

ISBN 978–1–4054–8800–6
Printed in China

CONTENTS

INTRODUCTION 10
Horses in Myth and Legend 14

DEVELOPMENT OF THE HORSE 18
The History of the Horse 20
Breeds and Types 22
Colours and Markings 23
Horses in Sport and Leisure 24

PONIES 26-81

LIGHT HORSES 82–193

HEAVY HORSES 194–225

TYPES 226–239

GLOSSARY 240–253

INTRODUCTION

T he horse has existed for millions of years and has played an important part in the progress of the human race. When man learned to ride he was transformed into a powerful being, able to see farther, move faster, and cover long distances more easily. The human power of reasoning combined with the horse's endurance and mobility made a formidable partnership – and since the horse lived in herds it found living with people easy and responded well to being domesticated. Over the years its contribution to our lives has been invaluable; it has provided transportation for both goods and people, as well as milk, meat and hides, and needs little in return. Horses can forage for their own food, will eat whatever is available, and can adapt to extremes of temperature and environment.

Aside from such practicalities, the horse is a beautiful animal and to watch the partnership of a good horse and rider is to see human and animal working as one. Anyone who has been lucky enough to see the famous Lipizzaners performing at the Spanish Riding School in Vienna will agree that it is a truly breathtaking experience. A well-schooled horse seems to anticipate what is required before it is asked for, and many horses learn to carry out basic tasks even without any input – delivery horses, for instance, soon learn where to stop on a regular round.

The Stud Book

Different breeds of horses are not as well defined as those of cats and dogs, for instance. This is partly because the horse has a much longer gestation period, so it takes a greater stretch of time to develop clearly defined characteristics, and horses have not been intensively bred for very long – most stud books are less than 100 years old.

A stud book registers the pedigree of a set breed of horse, recording its ancestry as far back as possible. Breeds that have a stud book have been selectively bred for long enough to have developed clearly defined characteristics. These will include an average size range, specific aspects of conformation, action and, in some breeds, a specific colour or range of colours.

There are two different types of stud book – open and closed. The closed type only allows new horses to be registered if both parents are already in that stud book, which means such breeds remain pure. Breeds with a closed stud book have very clear characteristics that can be transmitted without dilution down through following generations. The open stud book allows the entry of horses of different or mixed breeding as long as they are descended from pedigree parents. This allows breeders to adjust the breed as required, but can lead to the loss of clearly defined characteristics.

How this book is arranged

The breeds of horse fit into three main groups – ponies, light horses and heavy horses – and in addition there are types, which can be any breed. This book is arranged into these four sections (for further information on these, see page 22). Within the three groups the breeds of horse are listed by area of the world, then by country. The types of horse come at the end.

Left: A colourful fresco of horses and riders in Haveli, Rajasthan, India.

HORSES IN MYTH AND LEGEND

Not surprisingly, the horse features in many myths and legends. One of the most enduring stories is that of the Unicorn, which is found in different versions in many countries across the world. In the West, the Unicorn has traditionally been depicted as an elegant white horse with a long flowing mane and tail; its single horn projects from the centre of the forehead and is usually twisted and sometimes gold. The horn was supposed to neutralize poison and the animal's blood had a mystical power to heal, but the beast could only be caught and tamed by a virgin. However, in early illustrations the Unicorn looks more like a cross between a goat and a horse, with a bearded chin and cloven hooves. In Japan a similar legendary animal is called a *kirin*. In Roman times, Pliny described the Unicorn as having the body of a horse, head of a deer, feet of an elephant and tail of a boar, with a single black horn in the middle of its forehead. His Unicorn was a very fierce animal, with a bellowing voice, that could never be captured alive. Unlike the many fabulous beasts that were dangerous, the Unicorn was considered to be basically good.

The fabled Centaur was half man, half horse – usually the head and torso of a man and the body and legs of a horse. Centaurs were wild and lawless creatures, fond of drinking too much wine and carrying off beautiful maidens, although an exception was Chiron, a wise and gentle Centaur who was tutor to the Greek heroes Jason and Achilles. Centaurs feature in the stories of Heracles and in more modern times they appear in *The Chronicles of Narnia* by C.S. Lewis. and in *Harry Potter and the Order of the Phoenix* by J.K. Rowling, where they are antagonistic to both humans and wizards – although one, Firenze, becomes a tutor at Hogwarts.

Many stories of ancient deities include horses in some capacity. One well-known example is the Greek legend of Pegasus, a glorious winged horse who was the offspring of Poseidon, god of horses and of the sea, and Medusa, the snake-headed gorgon who could turn any living thing to stone with a single glance. When Medusa was killed by the Greek hero Perseus, Pegasus sprang fully formed from her body. Pegasus was later captured by Bellerophon, using a golden saddle given to him by Athena, goddess of wisdom, but when he tried to mount the magical horse Pegasus threw him off and galloped up to the heavens. In another version of the story, Bellerophon rode Pegasus to kill the evil Chimera, a monster with the

Right: A statue of Pegasus in Paris.

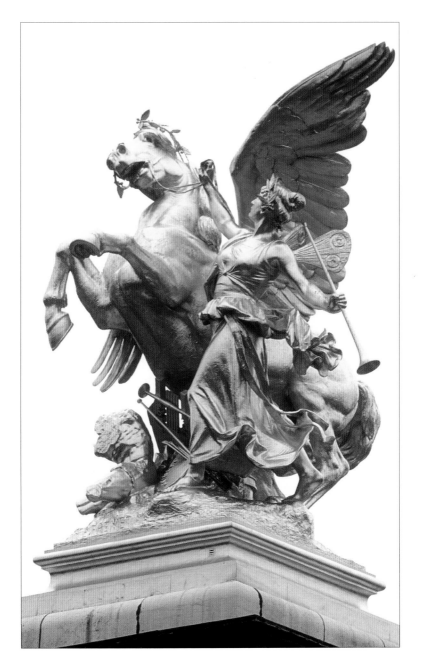

head of a lion, body of a goat and the tail of a dragon. After his success Bellerophon rode Pegasus to heaven to ask the gods for a favour, but enraged by his audacity Zeus sent a gadfly to sting Pegasus, who threw his rider and galloped away.

Horses are often connected with the heavens. In Norse legends, the goddess Sol rides across the sky each day in a chariot pulled by two horses, Arvak and Alsvid, and daylight comes not from the sun, but from the horses' manes. In Greek legend Helios, the sun god, drives a chariot from dawn to dusk pulled by four horses, Pyrios, Eos, Aethon and Phlegon. At night he is succeeded by his sister Selene, goddess of the moon, in a silver chariot pulled by two horses.

In many eras the horse has been connected to religion. The Uffington White Horse – a stylized outline of a horse cut through the grass on a British hillside to reveal the underlying chalk – dates back to the Iron Age and may be evidence of a horse cult. There are several similar horses across Great Britain, but most date from around the 18th century. Epona, goddess of horses, donkeys and mules, was worshipped across many areas of the world in Roman times, spread by the cavalry legions. She was also a goddess of fertility, so many representations of her include foals. The Four Horsemen of the Apocalypse are agents of destruction appearing in the Book of Revelation in the New Testament of the Bible. The first, on a white horse, symbolizes power or conquest, the second on a red horse brings violence or war, the third, on a black horse, means poverty or famine, and the fourth, on a pale horse, is Death.

There is also a famous imitation horse – the Trojan Horse, which appears in *The Aeneid*, an epic poem by Virgil about the Trojan war, and is also mentioned in Homer's *The Odyssey*. After laying siege to Troy for ten years without success, the Greeks built a hollow wooden horse, which they wheeled up to the gates of the city. They then appeared to leave, telling the Trojans the horse was a parting gift. Despite warnings from the soothsayer Cassandra, the Trojans opened the gates and took the horse into the city, before celebrating the end of the siege in some style. Early the following morning, while the Trojans were still in a drunken stupor, the hollow horse opened to reveal selected Greek warriors led by Odysseus hidden inside. They opened the city gates for the Greek army and Troy was defeated. Even now, a 'Trojan horse' is something that looks innocent but involves hidden trickery.

Left: A representation of the Wooden Horse of Troy.

DEVELOPMENT
OF THE
HORSE

THE HISTORY OF THE HORSE

The earliest example of a horse-type animal was the *Eohippus* – a small dog-like creature with four toes on its front feet and three on the back – which lived around 60 million years ago. Over the next 20 million years marshy ground began to give way to plains, and *Eohippus* adapted into *Mesohippus*, with three toes, and then *Merychippus*, with longer legs and a central toe. The first single-hoof type was *Pliohippus*, which emerged around six million years ago and had eyes on the side of its head for all-round vision and teeth suitable for grazing grasses. The zebra (*Equus zebra*), donkey (*Equus asinus*) and ass (*Equus hemionus hemionus*) are species also descended from *Pliohippus*, so they are related to the horse. The zebra is distributed throughout Southern Africa, the donkey originated in North Africa but has spread to many countries, and the ass is found in Asia and the Middle East.

The first true ancestor of the horse was *Equus caballus*, which dates from around one million years ago and resembled the more primitive horses of today. It was found in America, Europe and Asia, which were still connected by land bridges; when the land bridges disappeared after the last Ice Age the horse became extinct in America until it was reintroduced by the conquistadors. *Equus caballus* developed into three different types: *Equus Przewalskii Gmelini Antonius*, the Tarpan, ancestor of most light horse breeds and still found in Poland; *Equus Przewalskii Przewalskii Poliakov*, the Asiatic Wild Horse, or Przewalski's Horse which was rediscovered in 1881; and *Equus Silvaticus*, the Forest Horse, which is now extinct but was the ancestor of most heavy horses.

Further evolution is not clear, but it has been suggested that four subtypes developed before the horse was domesticated: Pony Type 1 from Northwest Europe, which resembled the Exmoor; Pony Type 2 from North Eurasia, which was heavier built with a convex profile and resembled Przewalski's Horse; Horse Type 3 from Central Asia, which was like the Akhal-Teke; and Horse Type 4 from Western Asia, which was probably the ancestor of the Arab. These types spread further afield as the use of the horse as a domestic animal increased.

Modern breeds have been developed using selective breeding to enhance desirable characteristics and they can be classified as either hot, warm or coldblood – for an explanation of these terms see page 22.

BREEDS AND TYPES

The different breeds of horse can be divided into Pony, Light Horse and Heavy Horse and although sometimes it is obvious to which category a particular breed belongs, some have less distinct characteristics.

Pony

Ponies are generally smaller than horses and their bodies are deep at the girth in relation to their height. Ponies tend to be sure-footed with a high knee action, and are very adaptable. They usually have lots of character but are quite placid.

Light Horse

Light Horse is a particularly broad term that covers horses that are suitable to ride, with backs that are not too broad and so take a saddle well. They move with a longer, lower action than the pony and the slope of the shoulders contributes to a smooth ride.

Heavy Horse

The Heavy Horse is large, well-built and heavily muscled and the legs often have heavy feathering of hair around the fetlock. The Heavy Horse has upright shoulders, which are better for fitting a collar, and its pulling power is ideal for ploughing, draught and carriage driving – although some breeds are also ridden.

Types

Types are horses that do not have a fixed breed, but which are particularly suitable for a purpose. Types include the Cob, Hunter, Polo Pony, Riding Pony and Hack.

Hot, Warm and Cold Blood

Horse breeds can be classified as having blood that is Hot, Warm or Cold. This is nothing to do with the actual temperature of the blood, but refers to ancestry and temperament. Hotbloods are active, fast, high-spirited horses, with a purity of breeding such as the Arab. Coldbloods are the heavy horses of Northern Europe, which are more placid and slow moving. Warmbloods are horses that combine hot and cold blood in various percentages.

COLOURS AND MARKINGS

There are thousands of possible combinations of coat colour and pattern in horses. Some breeds have set colours or patterns, others do not. Some of the more distinctive colours are described below.

Coat colours

Grey horses have black skin with white and black hairs, so a 'white' horse is actually called grey. Palomino horses have a solid gold coat with a white mane and tail

Patterns

Skewbald and piebald horses have coats that are patched in a colour and white. Piebald are black-and-white, skewbald are other colour and white – in North America this patterning is called pinto or paint. The Appaloosa is a spotted colouring in five set patterns – see pages 118–19.

Markings

The different markings on the face and legs can be used to identify a horse, along with patches of irregular coat hair called whorls. The star is a white diamond on the forehead – if it appears on the nose it is a snip. A narrow white line down the centre of the face is a stripe, but if it is wider it is a blaze. A horse can also have a completely white face, a white muzzle or white lip marks. White marks on the legs are: ermine, a narrow line above the hoof; sock, extending to the fetlock; and stocking, reaching to the knee.

Above: Markings on the coat are used to identify pedigree horses. From left to right, a star marking, a blaze and a white face.

HORSES IN SPORT AND LEISURE

Since horses were first domesticated pride has been taken in having the best or the fastest animal, so it was only natural that competitive events were soon set up. These now include competitions to test skill, speed and stamina – sometimes in a series of related events.

Racing

Horse racing as we know it today only really came into being after the Thoroughbred was developed in 17th century Britain. Many of the famous racecourses in Britain, such as Newmarket, were laid out at this time, after which the racing tradition quickly spread to America and New Zealand. In the 18th century racing became the first regulated sport in Britain, with the formation of the Jockey Club.

Driving

Modern harness racing is usually based mainly on elegance of style and movement, but can include a cross country section. In Europe, trotter racing is more common, in which the driver sits balanced on a light two-wheel sulky that is little more than a seat on a U-shaped shaft. Driving competitions date back for centuries – both the ancient Greeks and the Romans held chariot races.

Above: Dressage was originally developed by the cavalry to train their horses to respond instantly.
Opposite: Driving competitions have been popular for centuries.

Dressage

The cavalry originally developed dressage, a French term meaning training, as having a horse that responded instantly on command was invaluable in battle. In the 17th and 18th centuries dressage became fashionable, with displays like those still seen at the Spanish Riding School in Vienna. Dressage as a competitive sport developed in the 20th century.

Jumping

Showjumping also has military connections – cavalry horses were trained to jump over obstacles in the late 19th century.

Eventing

A comprehensive test of horse and rider, eventing includes three sections: dressage, cross-country racing and showjumping.

Leisure riding

Trekking and trail riding have become popular in many areas – they involve riding distances at a leisurely pace so are suitable for a range of skill levels.

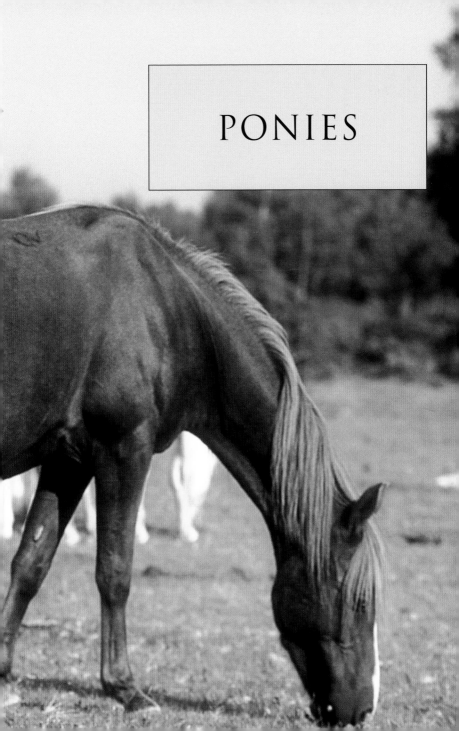

PONIES

BASUTO

Although the Basuto is one of the best known pony breed of South Africa, it is not indigenous. It is descended from horses brought into the Cape area in 1653 by the Dutch East India Company, which were the founders of the Cape Horse. Cape Horses were then taken over to Basutoland, after being captured as the spoils of war. While the Cape Horse evolved into a larger, more quality animal with the introduction of Thoroughbred and Arab blood, the Basuto interbred with local ponies and remained smaller and stockier. The Basuto achieved fame as a warhorse during the Boer War, but many of the best specimens were killed in the conflict. There has been a concerted effort to re-establish the breed, which is now not only used for general transport and racing but is also very popular with tourists for trekking holidays.

COUNTRY: Lesotho
BLOOD TEMPERATURE: Warm
HEIGHT: Up to 14.2 hands
COLOUR: Chestnut, brown, bay or grey, all with white markings
ENVIRONMENT: Rocky and hilly terrain
USES: Trekking, hacking, racing, polo
TEMPERAMENT: Docile, surefooted, brave
DESCRIPTION: Rather short legs, long straight back, muscular hindquarters, neat head on a long neck

NOOITGEDACHTER

COUNTRY: South Africa
BLOOD TEMPERATURE: Warm
HEIGHT: 13.2–15 hands
COLOUR: Bay, roan, chestnut
ENVIRONMENT: Transvaal
USES: Trekking, riding, jumping
TEMPERAMENT: Amiable, friendly
DESCRIPTION: Fine head, compact back with sloping shoulders, well-developed quarters, good legs, tough feet

The Nooitgedachter is descended from the Basuto, but also includes some Arab and Cape Horse blood. It is possibly the rarest horse breed in the world, as it is still only bred on a few hundred farms in Africa. By the 1940s the Basuto was in danger of extinction, so in 1951 the South African Department of Agriculture established a breeding stock of a few ponies at the Nooitgedachter Research Station in the eastern Transvaal. Here they followed a rigid breeding programme, keeping only the very best foals, to develop the new breed with all the excellent attributes of the Basuto including its hardy nature, surefootedness and love of human company. The Nooitgedachter is intelligent and easily trained and its tough feet seldom need to be shod, even on the roughest terrain. It is an excellent pony for children, but is also used for patrolling and trekking on game reserves.

MANIPURI

Believed to be descended from the Mongolian Wild Horse, crossed with oriental and Arab stock, the Manipuri is quite a small pony but is extremely quick, agile and tough. It became one of the original polo ponies when this fast-moving game was first introduced into Manipur by the ruling king in the 7th century. However, after the game spread across to Europe and America the height limit was gradually raised and now larger ponies are preferred. The breed was also used by the famed Manipur cavalry in the 17th century and as transport ponies by the British Army in Burma in the Second World War. Today the Manipuri is used in India both for polo and for racing and is also still employed by the military. The breed has a fast, long and low action as well as great stamina and intelligence.

COUNTRY: India
BLOOD TEMPERATURE: Warm
HEIGHT: Up to 13 hands
COLOUR: Bay, chestnut, grey, brown or pinto
ENVIRONMENT: Tropical
USES: Polo, racing
TEMPERAMENT: Intelligent, tough
DESCRIPTION: Compact body, broad chest, muscular hindquarters and neck, attractive head with broad muzzle, thick mane

SUMBA AND SUMBAWA

COUNTRY: Indonesia
BLOOD TEMPERATURE: Warm
HEIGHT: Up to 12.2 hands
COLOUR: Dun with black dorsal stripe and dark mane and tail
ENVIRONMENT: Barren tropics
USES: Pack, hacking, light draught
Temperament: Willing, quiet, sociable
DESCRIPTION: Rather primitive in looks, with large heavy head, short muscular neck, deep chest and long back

The Sumba and Sumbawa are essentially the same breed but are named after the respective neighbouring islands from which they originate. They are descended from primitive stock, but probably include both Chinese and Mongolian blood. The islands are harsh with poor grazing, so these horses are robust with good stamina and endurance. They resemble primitive ponies with heavy heads in proportion to the body and their dun colour, black dorsal stripe and darker mane and tail. However, unlike true primitives, they have a cooperative temperament and are both fast and agile. They are widely used on the islands as pack horses, for riding and light draught, and also in the fast and furious game of lance throwing. Some ponies are specially trained to dance – they wear bells at their knees and are ridden by young boys in patterns set by a dance master, moving in time to a rhythm beaten on a drum.

MONGOLIAN

Descended from the primitive Przewalski's Horse, the Mongolian is one of the oldest breeds in the world. It was probably the horse ridden by Ghengis Khan and his army as they swept through Asia and Europe and it retains many of its primitive characteristics. There are four main types, which differ according to the environmental conditions in which they developed. The largest is the forest type, which is most suitable for draught and pack work. The mountain and the steppes types are smaller, and more suitable for riding, while the desert, or Gobi type is the smallest. Some ponies are selectively bred for milk and meat. All the types look similar, with a rather coarse appearance, and they are extremely tough and famed for their stamina – they have been known to travel up to 120 miles (193 km) a day. Prized ponies also have a lateral gait, which is particularly smooth over long distances.

COUNTRY: Mongolia
BLOOD TEMPERATURE: Warm
HEIGHT: 12–14 hands
COLOUR: Dun, black, brown, chestnut, palomino
ENVIRONMENT: Forest, mountain, steppes and desert
USES: Draught, pack, hacking, also milk and meat
TEMPERAMENT: Phlegmatic, generally good disposition
DESCRIPTION: Short and stocky, muscular neck, relatively large head, short compact back, powerful hindquarters and short legs

AUSTRALIAN PONY

The Australian Pony has evolved from a mixture of the breeds imported by early settlers, since Australia has no indigenous breeds of horse. The imported horses mostly came initially from South Africa and Indonesia, but later British stock was used to develop the bloodline — most notably the Welsh Mountain Pony — as well as the Arab and Thoroughbred. The Australian Pony is excellent for children and novices because of its remarkably even temperament and good free action, but it also excels in jumping, dressage, gymkhana and pony club eventing. It is a strong animal, but also intelligent and attractive; it retains many of the traits of a Welsh Mountain Pony, with its compact body, neat head and large eyes. Although the legs are short, they are well shaped. All colours are accepted by the breed registry, except piebald and skewbald.

COUNTRY: Australia
BLOOD TEMPERATURE: Warm
HEIGHT: 12–14 hands
COLOUR: Can be any solid colour, but mostly grey
ENVIRONMENT: Temperate grassland
USES: Hacking, dressage, competitive driving
TEMPERAMENT: Easy-going, sociable
DESCRIPTION: Compact body with well-shaped head, arching neck, short straight back, deep chest and short strong legs

KONIK

Konik is the Polish word for 'little horse'. The Konik resembles the Huçul – the two horses originate from the same area of the world and are both believed to descend from the Tarpan, which died out in the 19th century. The addition of Arab blood at some point in its history has given the Konik some refinement and made it look more attractive. It is now selectively bred at the Polish state stud of Jezewice and at Popielno to maintain its breed characteristics. The Konik is tough and hardy, economical to keep and lives a long time, so it is widely used locally in agriculture, particularly in market gardening. It is now also very popular as a children's pony because of its docile temperament. Its high-set shoulders give it rather a poor action, but do make it good in harness.

COUNTRY: Poland
BLOOD TEMPERATURE: Warm
HEIGHT: Up to 13 hands
COLOUR: Greyish dun with dark dorsal stripe
ENVIRONMENT: Cool lowlands
USES: Hacking, light draught
TEMPERAMENT: Quiet, hardworking
DESCRIPTION: Well-proportioned head on a short muscular neck, upright shoulders, compact body, sturdy legs

CASPIAN

A miniature horse, the Caspian may be the most ancient breed in the world, dating back to 3000 BC. It was thought to be extinct but was rediscovered in Iran in 1965, when a small herd was found on the shores of the Caspian Sea. Some of these horses were taken to form the basis of the breed around the world, which has been carefully managed to retain the original characteristics. The Caspian looks like a miniature version of an Arab horse, with large eyes, a prominent jaw line and a high-set tail. Despite its tiny size it is very fast – able to keep up with much bigger horses – and is also an extremely good jumper. It has a wonderfully easy-going temperament, so it is ideal as a riding pony for children, and a long free-flowing stride that makes it very good as a show horse.

COUNTRY: Arabian peninsula
BLOOD TEMPERATURE: Hot
HEIGHT: Between 10–12 hands
COLOUR: Bay, chestnut, sometimes other solid colours
ENVIRONMENT: Desert
USES: Riding, harness
TEMPERAMENT: Very easy-going and sociable
DESCRIPTION: Small but well-proportioned, with attractive head on muscular neck, narrow back and strong quarters

GALICEÑO

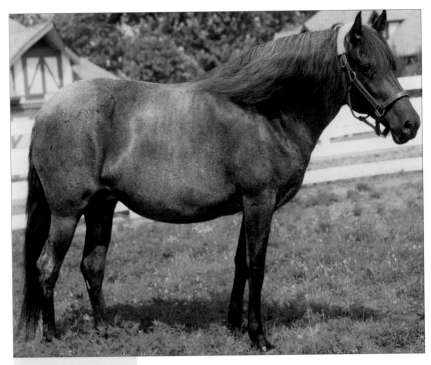

COUNTRY: Mexico
BLOOD TEMPERATURE: Warm
HEIGHT: Up to 14 hands
COLOUR: All solid colours
ENVIRONMENT: Savannah
USES: Riding, harness
TEMPERAMENT: Docile and gentle
DESCRIPTION: Finely built, with nicely proportioned head on a muscular arched neck, compact body, narrow chest and rather upright shoulders

Although the Galiceño developed in Mexico, it originated in northwest Spain – it is descended from the horses shipped to South America by Cortés in the 16th century; from Cuba he moved north into Mexico. The Galiceño is a tough and hardy breed, with a great deal of stamina and endurance, and a very distinctive running walk. This gives an exceptionally smooth gait that makes it very easy to ride, so it is believed to be ideal as an in-between mount for novices and children who are ready to graduate to horses. The Galiceño is intelligent, versatile, fast and quite easy to train and is widely used as a ranch horse as well as for riding, pack and light draught. Although it is relatively small it can carry a full-grown man over rough terrain throughout the heat of the day.

AMERICAN SHETLAND

The American Shetland is descended from the Scottish Shetland, which was imported into North America in 1885. It was later crossbred with Hackney ponies and small Arabs, so it now bears little resemblance to its ancestor. There are two distinct types to the American breed, with separate stud books – Division A contains only pure Shetlands, while Division B is for ponies with one parent from Division A and the other either a Hackney, Welsh or Harness show pony. The American Shetland is intelligent and versatile, as well as very tough and hardy, and is one of the most popular ponies in the United States. It has a good slope to its shoulders, and often has long legs, so exhibits quite an extravagant action, similar to the Hackney pony. It is very good at harness work, jumping and dressage and also makes an ideal children's pony because of its amiable nature.

COUNTRY: United States
BLOOD TEMPERATURE: Warm
HEIGHT: Up to 11.2 hands
COLOUR: All solid colours
ENVIRONMENT: Temperate open land
USES: Harness, trotting
TEMPERAMENT: Generally good
DESCRIPTION: Fine long head on a muscular arched neck, long narrow back, broad muscular hindquarters, long legs and luxurious mane and tail

AMERICAN WALKING PONY

COUNTRY: United States
BLOOD TEMPERATURE: Warm
HEIGHT: Up to 14 hands
COLOUR: All solid colours
ENVIRONMENT: Temperate climates
USES: Hacking, dressage, jumping, harness
TEMPERAMENT: Easy-going, sociable
DESCRIPTION: Fine head carried well on a muscular neck, broad deep chest, compact back, muscular hindquarters

A pony with the look of an Arab, the American Walking Pony was bred specifically to create a large and beautiful pony to perform in the show ring. It took many years to achieve the right combination, which involved a Tennessee Walking Horse crossed with a Welsh pony. The resulting breed has great presence and seven different gaits, including the Pleasure Walk, a four-beat gait faster than a walk but slower than a trot, and the Merry Walk, also a four-beat gait but faster and accompanied by a nodding head. The gaits were inherited from the Tennessee Walking Horse, but the canter of the American Walking Pony is also particularly smooth and unhurried and it is generally a comfortable horse to ride. Any solid colour is accepted by the breed registry, but the maximum height allowed is 14 hands.

ROCKY MOUNTAIN

One of the most recent breeds, the Rocky Mountain was developed in the late 1980s by Sam Tuttle of Stout Springs in Kentucky. He had the riding rights for the Natural Bridge State Park and found that riders of all ages and abilities were comfortable on his stallion Old Tobe, who had a sure-footed, four-beat gait. He bred a line of horses from Old Tobe, who not only inherited his gait, but were also sturdy and robust and had his calm and amiable nature. They have a great deal of stamina, being able to cover long distances even over rough terrain. They are not only popular with riders, but are versatile and can be used in light harness to pull buggies and carriages. Although the Rocky Mountain comes in many colours, the most prized is a deep chocolate with a flaxen mane and tail.

COUNTRY: United States
BLOOD TEMPERATURE: Warm
HEIGHT: 14.2–16 hands
COLOUR: All solid colours, no white on body
ENVIRONMENT: Temperate mountains
USES: Riding, trekking, harness
TEMPERAMENT: Easy-going, kind
DESCRIPTION: Intelligent head on a long graceful neck, deep wide neck, muscular shoulders, well-proportioned back

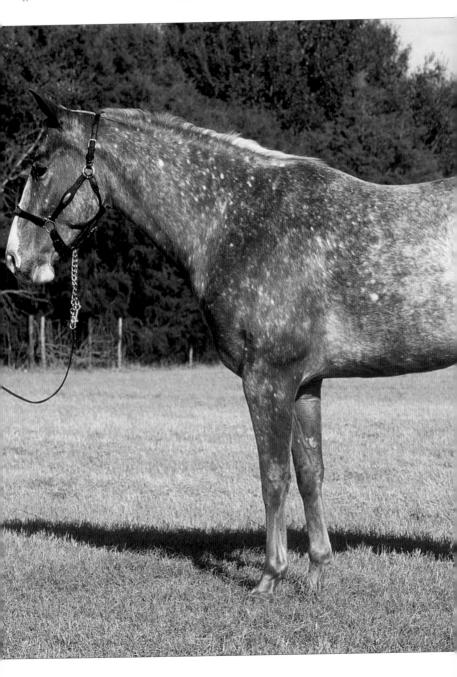

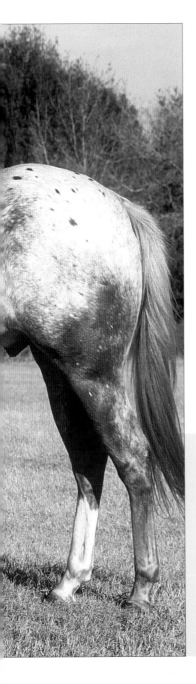

PONY OF THE AMERICAS

A recently developed breed, the Pony of the Americas is descended from a crossing between a Shetland and an Arab-Appaloosa in the early 1950s. The first colt had a distinctive black hand marking on one hindquarter, so was named Black Hand I. Later, Quarter Horse, Welsh and Arab blood were added and the breed standards were specifically set to make it the ideal mount for children. The official registry only accepts ponies with one of the recognized Appaloosa spotted coat patterns, and the height restrictions are also very strict. The Pony of the Americas is exceptionally gentle and quite easy to train and handle. It has a free-flowing and balanced action, which makes it an easy horse for a novice to ride, but it also has great presence in the show ring. It is one of the most popular ponies in the United States for children, but it is very versatile and is also often used for trail riding.

COUNTRY: United States
BLOOD TEMPERATURE: Warm
HEIGHT: 11.2–13.2 hands
COLOUR: Spotted in Appaloosa colours and patterns
ENVIRONMENT: Temperate grassland
USES: Hacking, trekking, show
TEMPERAMENT: Gentle and easy to train
DESCRIPTION: Fine head with a slightly concave profile on an arched neck, well-muscled body, sloping shoulders and tail carried high

HAFLINGER

COUNTRY: Austria
BLOOD TEMPERATURE: Cold
HEIGHT: Up to 15 hands
COLOUR: Chestnut with flaxen mane and tail
ENVIRONMENT: Mountain
USES: Pack, hacking, light draught, harness
TEMPERAMENT: Amiable
DESCRIPTION: Attractive head, broad strong back, powerful shoulders, muscled hindquarters, rather short legs

A mountain pony, the Haflinger is very attractive with its chestnut body – which can range from rust to light gold – set off by a flowing and abundant flaxen mane and tail. The breed is based on the now extinct Alpine Heavy Horse with the addition of Arab blood – although it is technically a coldblood – and takes its name from the village of Hafling in the Austrian Tyrol. The heritage of the Haflinger is particularly pure and careful monitoring of the breeding stock by the main stud at Jenesien ensures there is very little variation in characteristics. It is a very strong and sturdy pony, athletic, surefooted and intelligent. It has an attractive head, with a large eye and small upright ears, and a very amiable temperament, making it ideal for children and novices. It is also used in harness for pulling a sleigh or carriage.

DALES

The Dales pony is native to England and was originally developed as a pack pony – it is famous for its ability to carry heavy loads. It was used to transport lead ore from the mines of northern England, and later on small farms, where it was used for general tasks and ploughing. It is very similar to the Fell pony and probably descended from the same ancestor, but the Dales is more heavily built. Its breeding includes outcrosses to Welsh Cobs and the Clydesdale, but around 100 years ago a Welsh stallion was introduced into the programme, which gave the Dales a more free-flowing trot. It is also very surefooted and has a calm temperament, so although it was bred as a working pony it has become popular for riding and also excels in driving competitions. The full, flowing tail of the Dales often reaches the ground.

COUNTRY: Britain
BLOOD TEMPERATURE: Warm
HEIGHT: Up to 14.2 hands
COLOUR: Mainly black, sometimes dark brown or bay
ENVIRONMENT: Moorland
USES: Hacking, harness
TEMPERAMENT: Easy-going, sociable
DESCRIPTION: Powerful, muscular body, neat head, luxuriant mane and tail, thick silky feathering on lower legs

DARTMOOR

For centuries the Dartmoor pony lived semi-wild on the open moorlands of Dartmoor in Devon, but has faced extinction several times. Few pure-bred examples are to be seen there today, but the breed has been kept alive in private studs across the country, and in mainland Europe. Most modern ponies are descended via an Arab-bred stallion, The Leat, who was introduced into the breeding programme after the First World War. The Dartmoor is very athletic, with a natural jump and a good movement, so it makes a popular and elegant riding pony. It has an excellent disposition, sweet-tempered and willing, so it makes an ideal first pony – particularly for a child. Dartmoors also do well when driven in harness. The most acceptable colours are brown, bay or black with minimal white markings – skewbald and piebald ponies are not accepted into the breed register.

COUNTRY: Britain
BLOOD TEMPERATURE: Warm
HEIGHT: Up to 12.2 hands
COLOUR: Bay, brown, sometimes black
ENVIRONMENT: Moorland
USES: Hacking, harness
TEMPERAMENT: Easy-going, sociable
DESCRIPTION: Well-proportioned compact body, attractive head, muscular neck, full mane and tail

EXMOOR

COUNTRY: Britain
BLOOD TEMPERATURE: Warm
HEIGHT: 12–12.3 hands
COLOUR: Dun with black points, bay, brown
ENVIRONMENT: Moorland, mountain
USES: Hacking
TEMPERAMENT: Generally good disposition
DESCRIPTION: Compact body, wide forehead, hooded 'toad-eye' eyes, distinctive fan of hair at the top of the tail

The Exmoor is the oldest breed of horse in Britain – in fact it is probably one of the oldest in the world, as its jaw has a distinctive formation not found in other modern horse breeds but seen in fossilized bones. In general appearance it is very similar to horses seen in cave paintings of wild horses, so it may be an ancestor of the wild horse that has survived because of the isolation of its habitat. The Exmoor is extremely hardy and resistant to harsh weather, as well as to many equine diseases. Efforts to breed away from the Exmoor's natural habitat have not been successful, as descendants soon lose the breed's distinctive characteristics. Its waterproof winter coat has a woolly undercoat and a longer, greasy top coat that keeps the rain and cold out. The eyes have a heavy upper lid, known as a 'toad-eye', and there is an unusual fan-like growth of bushy hair at the top of the tail.

FELL

Both the Dales and the Fell pony probably developed from the same source – which was probably the now extinct Galloway, a fast and tough horse from Scotland. Another influence is thought to be the Friesian horse of Europe, which was used by Roman legions in Britain. The Fell was initially prized both as a strong riding horse that could easily carry a full-grown man all day and as a superb pack horse, used to carry lead, slate and copper to the docks. It has a smooth action and a fast walk that make it a comfortable ride, and is surefooted and placid. It is an ideal children's pony and is also excellent for hunting and driving in harness. The Fell has a particularly pure blood line – many white markings indicate a cross-bred pony that would not be accepted by the breed registry.

COUNTRY: Britain
BLOOD TEMPERATURE: Warm
HEIGHT: Up to 14 hands
COLOUR: Usually black, also brown, bay and grey
ENVIRONMENT: Moorland
USES: Riding, harness, pack
TEMPERAMENT: Easy-going, calm disposition
DESCRIPTION: Small neat head on a long neck, strong body, muscular quarters, prolific mane and tail, feathering on legs

HACKNEY

In the 19th century, the Hackney pony was developed by Christopher Wilson in Cumbria in the north of Britain. He based the new breed on the Fell pony, with some Welsh blood, to create a show pony with an extravagant high-stepping action. The ponies were traditionally kept out on the fells over winter and left to fend for themselves, which developed toughness and endurance in the breed and kept the animals quite small. The Hackney is a very elegant pony, with a fine silky coat, and the toes are often allowed to grow longer than normal to accentuate its snappy action. Mainly used for show driving, the Hackney has a spectacular fluid action and carries its tail high and its neck arched. Its exuberance in the show ring creates an exciting display. The Hackney pony shares the same stud book as the Hackney horse, a larger and older breed.

COUNTRY: Britain
BLOOD TEMPERATURE: Warm
HEIGHT: 12.2–14 hands
COLOUR: All solid colours
ENVIRONMENT: Moorland
USES: Harness
TEMPERAMENT: Generally good
DESCRIPTION: Small, well-shaped head on muscular arched neck, powerful shoulders and quarters, high-set tail

HIGHLAND

COUNTRY: Britain
BLOOD TEMPERATURE: Warm
HEIGHT: Up to 14.2 hands
COLOUR: All colours
ENVIRONMENT: Cool highlands
USES: Riding, harness, pack
TEMPERAMENT: Easy-going, biddable
DESCRIPTION: Sturdy, attractive head on long neck, deep and powerful chest, muscular hindquarters, short legs

A mixture of many breeds – including French ponies, Spanish horses, Fell and Dales ponies and Arabs – the Highland has been developed over centuries. Its harsh environment means the breed is very tough and can tolerate extremely bad weather; it is also very strong, agile and docile. It is economical to keep and generally free from any hereditary equine diseases. The Highland was traditionally used as a pack horse, as well as for riding and agriculture by crofters, and was known for its ability to cross wet ground – even when covered with quite deep water. It is now often used for forestry work and for trekking, as well as general riding for all abilities. It is also used to carry deer carcasses down from the hills after the herds are culled. The Highland comes in all solid colours, including dun with a black dorsal stripe, but white markings are usually minimal.

LUNDY PONY

A fairly recent breed, the Lundy Pony was developed on the island of Lundy, off the southwest coast of Britain, but in the 1980s the herd was moved to the mainland to the county of Cornwall and then also to Devon. The Lundy is based on a cross between the New Forest pony and the Arab, with later infusions of blood from Connemara and Welsh Mountain ponies. Lundy is a fairly harsh environment as the grazing is often quite poor and the weather can be extreme, so the Lundy Pony developed into a hardy breed and is economical to feed. Its good nature and fairly small stature make it an ideal pony for children; it is also a good jumper. Some ponies were later returned to Lundy and now live wild in a small herd on the island.

COUNTRY: Britain
BLOOD TEMPERATURE: Warm
HEIGHT: Up to 13.2 hands
COLOUR: Dun, roan, liver chestnut, bay palomino
ENVIRONMENT: Barren temperate
USES: Riding
TEMPERAMENT: Generally good-natured
DESCRIPTION: Fine head on a muscular neck, well-proportioned compact body with deep chest and good quarters

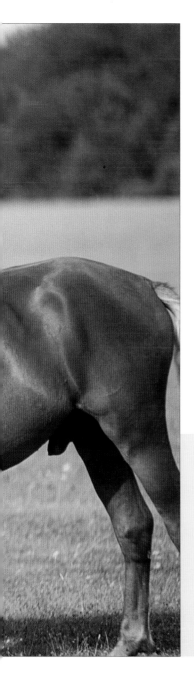

NEW FOREST

The New Forest pony has lived in a semi-wild state in the New Forest in Hampshire, in the south of England, since the 10th century. It is one of the biggest pony breeds in Britain and is extremely versatile so quite a number are now bred in studs, although there are still many roaming free in the forest. The breed's origins are not known, but Welsh ponies were introduced to the herds in 1208 and a Thoroughbred stallion in 1765, as well as an Arab and a Barb stallion lent by Queen Victoria herself in the late 19th century. Although Fell, Dales, Dartmoor, Highland, Welsh and Exmoor ponies were all used to improve the stock towards the end of the 19th century, the New Forest pony has retained its own characteristics. It has a hardy nature and an easy action, and is used for riding, dressage, harness and jumping. Its amiable nature makes it a great mount for children, but it can easily carry an adult.

COUNTRY: Britain
BLOOD TEMPERATURE: Warm
HEIGHT: 12–14.2 hands
COLOUR: All solid, mostly bay or brown
ENVIRONMENT: Moorland
USES: Riding, harness, dressage
TEMPERAMENT: Easy-going, friendly
DESCRIPTION: Attractive horse-like head, well-proportioned body, muscular neck and hindquarters, finely shaped legs

SHETLAND

Although it is quite tiny – its size is measured in centimetres or inches, rather than hands – the Shetland is a powerful pony that can carry a full-grown adult. The inhospitable habitat of its original home, the Shetland islands off the coast of Scotland, have influenced its small stature but have also made the breed hardy, resistant to poor weather and long-lived. The first ponies may have been brought by the Vikings, or perhaps crossed from Scandinavia before the islands were separated from mainland Europe. They are one of the oldest British breeds and have changed very little in appearance over the years. When children were no longer allowed to work in mines the Shetland provided a suitable substitute, but these days it is most often used as a children's starter pony or just as a pet. All coat colours are accepted, except spotted.

COUNTRY: Britain
BLOOD TEMPERATURE: Warm
HEIGHT: Up to 102 cm (40 in.)
COLOUR: All colours, including piebald and skewbald
ENVIRONMENT: Barren temperate
USES: Riding, harness
TEMPERAMENT: Gentle, sociable
DESCRIPTION: Diminutive but well-proportioned, small head, short neck, deep girth, short legs, full mane and tail

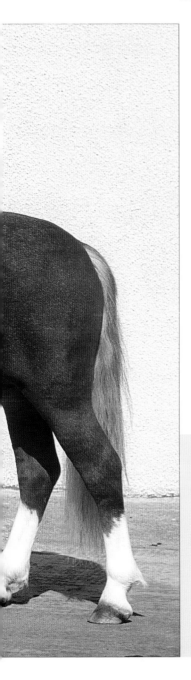

WELSH MOUNTAIN

The Welsh Mountain pony (Section A) is perhaps the most numerous of the native British breeds. It was recorded in Roman times and has benefited over the years from the influx of oriental blood, as well as Arab, Thoroughbred and Hackney. The Arab part of its heritage has given it attractive looks, with a small, concave head, neat face and large eyes. The Welsh Mountain is the smallest of the Welsh breeds, and is also the foundation from which the other three have derived. It has a wonderfully gentle temperament, which makes it ideal as a children's pony, but is also very strong, intelligent and talented when used in harness. The harsh environment of its origins created a pony with endurance, surefootedness and a sound constitution, qualities that have endured in the breed today. It is also quite economical to feed.

COUNTRY: Britain
BLOOD TEMPERATURE: Warm
HEIGHT: Up to 12 hands
COLOUR: All colours except piebald and skewbald
ENVIRONMENT: Mountain, moorland
USES: Riding, harness
TEMPERAMENT: Easy-going, calm, gentle
DESCRIPTION: Arab-like head on arched neck, deep chest, short back, good width at girth, muscular quarters and well-shaped legs

WELSH COB

COUNTRY: Britain
BLOOD TEMPERATURE: Warm
HEIGHT: Up to 13.2 hands
COLOUR: All colours except piebald and skewbald
ENVIRONMENT: Moorland, mountain
USES: Riding, trekking, harness
TEMPERAMENT: Easy-going, friendly
DESCRIPTION: Attractive head on a muscular arched neck, compact body with deep chest, good width at girth and muscular quarters

There are three types of Welsh pony with different sections in the stud book, plus Section D – the Welsh Cob – which is bigger and is normally classed as a horse. The Cob type pony is in Section C and is very versatile, with the best characteristics of the Welsh Mountain but slightly bigger and heavier. In the 12th century both Sections C and D almost certainly evolved after Welsh Mountain ponies were crossed with horses brought over by the Romans, with infusions of Spanish blood and later Norfolk Trotter and Hackney. The Welsh Cob type ponies were used on farms for all kinds of work, and in the local slate mines. These days they are mostly used for riding, particularly trekking, but are also very good in harness and are excellent jumpers. Since the Welsh Cob type is hardy and used to living outside all year round, it is very economical to keep.

WELSH PONY

Although it retains all the good characteristics of the Welsh Mountain pony, the Welsh Pony is a little larger but has a lighter build and a lower, smoother action, so is more versatile. Like the other Welsh types, it is based on the Welsh Mountain, crossed with Arab, Barb and probably the Welsh Cob. The Welsh Pony is an excellent jumper and its free-flowing action makes it quite eye-catching in the show ring. It also has the natural balance and rhythm needed for dressage as well as being very good in harness, so it is the perfect all-rounder and ideal for a young rider. Like the other Welsh breeds, it is accepted in all colours except piebald and skewbald. Welsh ponies have been exported around the world and there are now breed societies as far afield as America and Australia.

COUNTRY: Britain
BLOOD TEMPERATURE: Warm
HEIGHT: Up to 13.2 hands
COLOUR: All colours except piebald and skewbald
ENVIRONMENT: Mountain, moorland
USES: Riding, harness, dressage
TEMPERAMENT: Easy-going, calm, gentle
DESCRIPTION: Attractive head with broad forehead tapering to a fine muzzle, gently arched neck, well-proportioned body, tail carried high

ARIÉGEOIS

This ancient French breed is also known as Cheval de Mérens, but its better-known name of Ariégeois comes from the Ariège river in the eastern Pyrenees. Its looks appear to have changed little over the centuries, as cave paintings have been found in the region showing very similar animals. The Ariégeois is a hardy mountain breed and is at home in ice and snow, although it does not fare well in the heat. It was traditionally used mainly as a pack pony – particularly by smugglers working across the mountains between France and Spain – as well as on local hill farms and in mines, and is usually unshod even on rough mountain tracks. Its coat is pure black, generally without any white markings at all – although it can show rust-coloured highlights in winter. Since it has a sweet nature, it is now often used for riding.

COUNTRY: France
BLOOD TEMPERATURE: Cold
HEIGHT: 13.1–14.3 hands
COLOUR: Black
ENVIRONMENT: Mountain
USES: Pack, light draught, riding
TEMPERAMENT: Amiable, easy-going
DESCRIPTION: Attractive head on a short muscular neck, stocky body with deep chest and straight shoulders, low-set tail, thick forelock and mane

FRENCH SADDLE PONY

COUNTRY: France
BLOOD TEMPERATURE: Warm
HEIGHT: 12.2–14.2 hands
COLOUR: All colours
ENVIRONMENT: Temperate areas
USES: Riding
TEMPERAMENT: Generally sweet natured
DESCRIPTION: Small fine head on a medium length neck, deep and wide chest, sloping shoulders, straight back and strong legs

A relatively new breed, the French Saddle pony – Poney Français de Selle – was created in France to fulfil the same need as the British Riding Pony, as a versatile show pony for children. It is also sometimes called the French Riding Pony. The breeding programme used native French ponies and horses, including the Landais and the Selle Français, crossed with Welsh, New Forest and Arab bloodlines. The result is a very attractive pony with a fine head, large eyes and alert ears. The body is well-proportioned and the tail is carried high so the animal looks good in the show ring. Its temperament is generally calm and amiable, although some ponies are a little lively and can be highly strung. Because of the mix of breeds used to create it, the French Saddle Pony comes in all colours, including piebald and skewbald.

LANDAIS

Although it is a very old French breed – dating back to the 8th century – the Landais has been heavily influenced by breeds from other parts of the world, including the Arab, Barb and Welsh. It is named after its region of origin, the forested Landes area in southwest France. There was also once a similar but bigger and heavier horse originating in the same area, which was called the Barthais, but the two breeds merged at some point to become one. Originally the Landais was a pack animal or used for light draught, since although it was lightly built it was very strong and hardy. Later it was used in the development of the French Saddle Pony and is now often used as a pony for children, because of its intelligent, quiet and kind nature. There are very few purebred Landais left, so efforts are being made to preserve the breed.

COUNTRY: France
BLOOD TEMPERATURE: Warm
HEIGHT: 11.3–13.1 hands
COLOUR: Bay, brown, chestnut, black
ENVIRONMENT: Temperate
USES: Riding, harness
TEMPERAMENT: Usually easy-going, can be wilful
DESCRIPTION: Small head with a broad forehead and straight profile, muscular neck, sloping shoulders, short wide back, sloping hindquarters

POTTOCK OR BASQUE

COUNTRY: France
BLOOD TEMPERATURE: Warm
HEIGHT: 11–14.2 hands
COLOUR: All colours except grey
ENVIRONMENT: Mountain
USES: Pack, light draught, riding
TEMPERAMENT: Sweet natured, willing
DESCRIPTION: Well-proportioned head, with either concave or straight profile, large eyes, heavy shoulders, wide chest and long back

The Pottock comes from the Basque region of southwest France, so is also sometimes called the Basque pony. It is an ancient mountain breed, probably descended from the now extinct Tarpan, and can look rather unprepossessing – although attempts have been made to improve the breed using Arab and Welsh blood. There are still wild herds of purebred Pottock ponies in the Basque region, some of which are rounded up each year to be sold. Since its qualities of endurance, strength and resourcefulness are now appreciated much more, Pottocks are also bred in studs – and these are generally a better quality animal. The Pottock is athletic, hardy and surefooted and has often been employed for pack and light draught work. It is also now often used for riding and its sweet nature makes it particularly suitable for children.

ICELANDIC

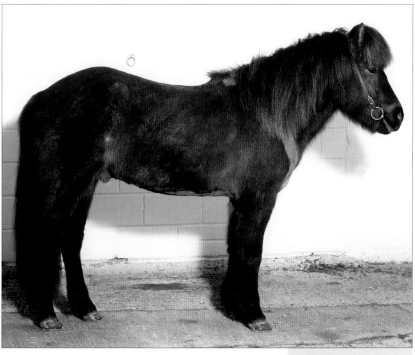

The Icelandic horse is very small in stature so it is technically a pony although it is called a horse. It is not indigenous to Iceland and is believed to have descended from livestock brought to the island by the Vikings in the 9th century, which probably included such breeds as the Forest Pony of Europe and the Tarpan. The Icelandic has a particularly pure bloodline, as no other breeds have been introduced for over 900 years, since a disastrous attempt to add Arab blood. This had a detrimental effect on the native horse so laws were passed ensuring that foreign breeds could not be imported, which are still in effect even today. The Icelandic is used for all types of work on the island. It has five natural gaits – walk, trot, gallop, pace and the *tölt*. The pace is a two-beat lateral gait that is only used over short distances, while the *tölt* is a unique, fast, four-beat running walk.

COUNTRY: Iceland
BLOOD TEMPERATURE: Warm
HEIGHT: 12.3–13.2 hands
COLOUR: All colours
ENVIRONMENT: Tundra
USES: Riding, harness, light draught
TEMPERAMENT: Usually placid, sometimes temperamental
DESCRIPTION: Large head on a short thick neck, sturdy body, strong legs, thick mane and forelock

CONNEMARA

An old breed native to the moorland and mountainous bogs in the west of Ireland, the Connemara is descended from the Celtic pony. It was once used by local farmers, carrying out all the general work on the farm. Spanish Jennet and Barb horses, as well as Arab, Welsh Cobs and Thoroughbreds, have all been used in the breeding programme over the years and the result is a good-looking, talented pony that is athletic, agile and a superb jumper. The Connemara also has an even temperament, is very intelligent and is resistant to adverse weather conditions. Originally their coats were dun coloured with a black dorsal stripe and black points, but now they tend to be grey or sometimes bay or brown. Connemaras make excellent competition ponies, not just for show jumping but also for dressage, eventing and competitive driving. They are excellent as a pony for beginners and are large enough to be ridden by older children and light adults.

COUNTRY: Ireland
BLOOD TEMPERATURE: Warm
HEIGHT: 13–14.2 hands
COLOUR: Grey, dun, bay, brown, chestnut, roan
ENVIRONMENT: Boggy moorland
USES: Hacking, harness
TEMPERAMENT: Easy-going, sociable
DESCRIPTION: Compact body, deep broad chest, fine neat head, a well-arched neck and powerful hindquarters

FJORD

COUNTRY: Norway
BLOOD TEMPERATURE: Warm
HEIGHT: 13–14.2 hands
COLOUR: Dun with lighter tail and two-tone mane, dark dorsal stripe
ENVIRONMENT: Taiga
USES: Riding, harness, pack
TEMPERAMENT: Usually placid, can be wilful
DESCRIPTION: Neat head on a powerful neck, stocky body, short strong legs, two-tone mane with a dark centre and lighter outside hairs

An ancient breed, the Norwegian Fjord has very primitive characteristics and strongly resembles the Asian Wild Horse, now known as Przewalski's Horse. The Fjord was ridden by the Vikings and travelled with them in their longboats to many other areas of the world. Since Viking times, the coarse two-tone mane has traditionally been trimmed so the central black hair stands upright, lined on each side with the shorter silvery-white hair. The coat is always dun, in various shades, with a darker dorsal stripe, and the tail is thick and full. The Fjord is a stocky, compact pony, very powerful but also quite graceful. It is an excellent worker and is very versatile – it is often used on hill farms for ploughing, as well as for general driving. Some are also ridden, as the breed's gentle and willing nature makes it suitable for all levels of skill.

GARRANO

The Garrano is the Portuguese equivalent of the more famous Sorraia, which is found in neighbouring Spain, but its bloodline is not as pure. It is an ancient breed, but a considerable influx of foreign blood – mainly Arab – has diluted some of its primitive features. It originates in the fertile but mountainous region of the Minho province, so its alternative name is the Minho. The Garrano is believed by some to be an ancestor of both the Galiceno and the Andalusian. It is a hardy breed, very strong and usually with a calm temperament – although some animals are rather highly strung. It is surefooted and can travel easily over the steep tracks through thick woodland that are a feature of its homeland, so it was once used as a pack animal, particularly by the military. It is very fast for its size, so often competes in trotting races; it is also ridden and used for light farm work.

COUNTRY: Portugal
BLOOD TEMPERATURE: Warm
HEIGHT: 10–14 hands
COLOUR: Bay, sometimes brown or chestnut
ENVIRONMENT: Temperate woodlands
USES: Harness, light draught, riding, pack
TEMPERAMENT: Generally calm, can be highly strung
DESCRIPTION: Attractive head, sometimes with concave profile, long neck, compact body with deep chest and sloping muscular quarters, short legs

FALABELLA

Miniature horses such as the Falabella were originally bred as curiosities and as pets. Their size is not due to environmental conditions, but to selective breeding – continually choosing the smallest animals and breeding them to each other. Although a selection of naturally small ponies were used in the programme – such as Shetlands, a small English Thoroughbred and a Criollo – the inbreeding to take the Falabella down to its tiny size (measured in centimetres rather than in hands) has meant that it is quite likely to suffer conformational defects such as weak hocks, a heavy head or crooked limbs. However, the best examples are perfect miniature horses, with an intelligent and friendly nature. They are long-lived, often surviving past 40 years. Due to its reduced stature the Falabella is not suitable for riding – except by the smallest child – but is quite strong for its size and has been driven in harness.

COUNTRY: Argentina
BLOOD TEMPERATURE: Warm
HEIGHT: 76–82.5 cm (30–33 in)
COLOUR: All colours
ENVIRONMENT: Temperate
USES: Novelty
TEMPERAMENT: Generally calm
DESCRIPTION: Proportionally large head, compact body, straight shoulders, luxuriant mane and tail

PINDOS

COUNTRY: Greece
BLOOD TEMPERATURE: Warm
HEIGHT: Up to 13 hands
COLOUR: Bay, black, brown, grey
ENVIRONMENT: Mountain
USES: Riding, harness, light draught, pack
TEMPERAMENT: Generally calm but can be stubborn
DESCRIPTION: Rather coarse head on a medium length neck, narrow body with underdeveloped quarters, fine-boned legs, high-set tail

The origins of the Pindos pony are unclear, but it may be descended from the ancient Thessalonian breed with some influx of Arab blood. Its homeland is infertile and is extremely hot in summer and very cold in winter, but the Pindos has adapted well to these harsh conditions and is very hardy, long-lived and able to survive for considerable periods on minimal rations. Its hard feet are rarely shod, even though it regularly has to negotiate stony mountain tracks. Although it may not be the most attractive of equine breeds, its stamina means that it is valued as a workhorse, being used locally on small farms, as a pack animal and for riding. Mares are sometimes used to breed excellent mules, which are very hardworking and cheap to keep. The Pindos does have a reputation for being rather difficult and stubborn.

BARDIGIANO

The Bardigiano is not very well known outside its native Italy, but it is closely related to the Avelignese and the Haflinger and resembles the British Exmoor pony. It comes from the northern Appenine region of Italy and is a working pony, often still used to carry packs in mountainous areas of its homeland. It is strong and hardy, quite fast but surefooted, economical and easy to keep. It has a quiet and generally amiable temperament, making it ideal for trekking as well as light agricultural work. During both the First and the Second World Wars, Bardigianos were used to breed excellent mules, but this gradually reduced the number of purebred animals available. In the 1970s, efforts were made to re-establish the original breed – these have been quite successful, but numbers are still very small and its survival remains in danger.

COUNTRY: Italy
BLOOD TEMPERATURE: Warm
HEIGHT: Up to 13 hands
COLOUR: All solid colours, but mostly bay
ENVIRONMENT: Temperate mountains
USES: Pack, light draught
TEMPERAMENT: Easy-going
DESCRIPTION: Attractive pony-type head on a muscular neck, powerful upright shoulders, compact body, muscular quarters, profuse mane and tail

AVELIGNESE

The Italian version of the Haflinger, the Avelignese takes its name from Avelengo in the mountainous Alto Adige region on Italy's border with Austria. The two breeds bear a great resemblance to each other and are both thought to be descended from Arab horses bred to the now extinct Alpine Heavy Horse. The Avelignese is now widely bred throughout Italy since it is hardworking, tough and enduring, partly due to the harsh mountain environment from which it originated. It is larger than the Haflinger and is very versatile – it is still used for agricultural work and as a pack horse, but has also become the ideal mount for trekking because it is so surefooted and calm. Although they are quite large, easily capable of carrying an adult, they are often used as mounts for children or for nervous riders.

COUNTRY: Italy
BLOOD TEMPERATURE: Cold
HEIGHT: Up to 14.3 hands
COLOUR: Chestnut with flaxen mane and tail
ENVIRONMENT: Mountains
USES: Harness, pack, riding
TEMPERAMENT: Placid, good natured
DESCRIPTION: Fine head with broad forehead tapering to a neat muzzle, short muscular neck, powerful upright shoulders, broad chest, muscular quarters, feathered fetlocks

SORRAIA

Another descendant of the ancient Tarpan breed, the Sorraia still has many primitive characteristics and resembles the horses shown in prehistoric cave paintings. It originates from the plains of Portugal, between the rivers Sor and Raia in the western region of the Iberian peninsula. Although its looks are not particularly attractive, the Sorraia is agile, intelligent and easy to train, so it was traditionally used by Spanish cowboys to herd livestock as well as to work the land. There are few purebreds left today, but a small feral herd is maintained by the d'Andrade family on their estate in Portugal. The influence of the Sorraia can be seen in some American breeds, such as the Mustang, as the Spanish took horses to the New World. It is also one of the ancestors of the Spanish Andalusian and Lusitano breeds

COUNTRY: Portugal
BLOOD TEMPERATURE: Warm
HEIGHT: Up to 13 hands
COLOUR: Grey-dun with black mane and tail
ENVIRONMENT: Temperate plains
USES: Feral, harness, riding
TEMPERAMENT: Easy-going, amiable
DESCRIPTION: Heavy head with convex profile on elegant muscular neck, compact body with straight shoulders, deep chest and sloping quarters

LIGHT HORSES

BARB

Like the Arab, the Barb is an ancient breed that has had a tremendous influence on many later breeds of horse. Both are desert horses – the Barb comes from northwest Africa – so they have great endurance, but the Barb is not as graceful nor as attractive as the Arab. However, the Barb is particularly renowned for its great stamina, agility and speed over short distances and was once greatly valued as a warhorse. Its exact origins are unclear – some believe that it was a wild horse that survived the Ice Age. It is certainly clear that Barb genes are very dominant, as it has retained its basic characteristics over centuries. The Barb spread into Spain, France and Portugal as the mount of the marauding Berbers, and its blood can be seen in the Andalusian, the Lusitano, the famous white Camargue horses – and even in the British Thoroughbred and the American Mustang.

COUNTRY: Morocco
BLOOD TEMPERATURE: Hot
HEIGHT: 14.15.2 hands
COLOUR: Chestnut, black, grey bay
ENVIRONMENT: Desert
USES: Riding
TEMPERAMENT: Highly strung and temperamental
DESCRIPTION: Narrow head, often with convex profile, muscular neck, straight shoulders, deep chest, sloping quarters, low-set tail

INDIAN HALF-BRED

COUNTRY: India
BLOOD TEMPERATURE: Warm
HEIGHT: 15–16 hands
COLOUR: All colours
ENVIRONMENT: Tropical
USES: Riding
TEMPERAMENT: Good natured
DESCRIPTION: Fine head, sometimes with curving ears, nicely sloping shoulders, deep chest, straight back, well-formed quarters and strong legs

Descended from a cross between the Kathiawari and the Australian Waler, with Arab and Thoroughbred blood added, the Indian Half-bred was specifically bred at army studs as a cavalry horse. The climate of India is harsh and the grazing tends to be poor, but the Indian Half-bred can easily cope with these conditions and is both hardy and an economical feeder, while its foreign ancestors have made it larger and more refined than the native stock. Until the military was mechanized the Indian Half-bred was used as the main method of transport, and even now it is still used as a pack horse and for the few remaining mounted divisions. It is also used by mounted police in many areas, particularly in rural regions, while civilian riding clubs sometimes utilize it as a competition horse, since it is intelligent and willing.

KATHIAWARI

The Kathiawari takes its name from the Kathwiar peninsula on India's west coast. The breed dates back to the 14th century, possibly originating as a cross between local ponies and Arabs – either imported or, more romantically, that had swum ashore from a shipwreck. The Kathiawari has many Arab characteristics and is highly prized in its homeland. It has a natural pace, indicating that central Asian breeds may have played some part in its heritage. It was once bred only by princely families, but most now come from the government stud at Junagadh. In the 19th century the Kathiawari gained renown as a warhorse used by both the British and Indian cavalries. Today its agility and speed make it ideal for polo and it is also a favoured mount for the local fast game of tent-pegging. In some areas of India it is also used by mounted police.

COUNTRY: India
BLOOD TEMPERATURE: Hot
HEIGHT: Up to 15 hands
COLOUR: Usually chestnut, but any solid colour except black
ENVIRONMENT: Tropical
USES: Riding, polo
TEMPERAMENT: Usually placid, can be temperamental
DESCRIPTION: Fine head with distinctive ears that curve round to touch at the tips, graceful neck, slim wiry body, sloping shoulders, deep chest, slim legs

MARWARI

COUNTRY: India
BLOOD TEMPERATURE: Hot
HEIGHT: Average 14.3, but can reach 16 hands
COLOUR: All colours
ENVIRONMENT: Tropical
USES: Riding
TEMPERAMENT: Loyal, generally good temperament
DESCRIPTION: Long head with distinctive ears curving round to touch at the tip, muscular neck, well-built compact body, sloping shoulders, long legs

Although it is usually quite small, the Marwari is classed as a horse not a pony. Its origins are not clear, but it probably developed in the same way as a nearby breed, the Kathiawari. The Marwari was also used as a warhorse, and had a reputation for particular bravery in battle – it was said that even if injured it would carry its rider to safety and if its rider fell it would stand guard over him. The famous Imperial Cavalry of Rajput mainly rode Marwari steeds in the 16–17th centuries and they were also used in the First World War. Later numbers began to decline, and by the 1930s the breed was almost extinct, until the Maharajah of Jodhpur took an interest and began a breeding programme. Today the Marwari is enjoying a revival, supported both by the government and the Marwari Breeders' Association.

AKHAL-TEKE

Images of the Akhal-Teke have been found dating back to the 9th century BC, which makes the breed older than the Arab. It was favoured by Alexander the Great, Genghis Khan and Marco Polo as a mount that could not only survive harsh conditions but had exceptional endurance over long distances. Its exact origins are unknown, but it comes from the region of the Kara Kum desert in Turkmenistan and gets its name from the oasis of Akhal in the Kopet Dag mountains and the Teke tribe, which lived there. With the extremes of heat and cold and poor grazing here for much of the year, the Akhal-Teke developed into a tough horse with a great deal of stamina. Traditionally it was bred for racing, and today it also excels at jumping and dressage. A notable feature of the Akhal-Teke is the unusual metallic sheen of its coat.

COUNTRY: Turkmenistan
BLOOD TEMPERATURE: Hot
HEIGHT: 14.2–15.2 hands
COLOUR: Chestnut, dun, palomino, bay or grey
ENVIRONMENT: Desert
USES: Riding, dressage
TEMPERAMENT: Usually placid, can be temperamental
DESCRIPTION: Finely modelled head on long muscular neck, slender body with deep but narrow chest and sloping shoulders, muscular quarters, long legs

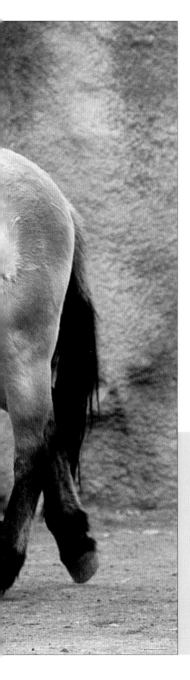

PRZEWALSKI'S HORSE

For many years the Asian Wild Horse was believed to be extinct after it was hunted in the wild for meat. However, in 1881 the Russian Colonel Nikolai Przewalski discovered two small wild herds living in the Tachin Schara Nuhu mountains in Mongolia near the Gobi desert. The rediscovered breed was named after the Colonel and some of the horses were later captured and kept in zoos and at research stations. After the wild herds had apparently died out, the zoo animals were carefully bred to retain the best stock and a small herd was reintroduced into the wild, in Hustain Nuruu, a small nature reserve in the Mongolian steppes. The Przewalski is the only known true wild horse in the world and is generally accepted to be one of the ancestors of the modern horse – although some contend that it is a separate species as it has 66 chromosomes, while all other breeds of horse have only 64.

COUNTRY: Mongolia
BLOOD TEMPERATURE: Warm
HEIGHT: Up to 14.2 hands
COLOUR: Dun with dark dorsal stripe
ENVIRONMENT: Steppes, taiga
USES: Feral
TEMPERAMENT: Stubborn and aggressive
DESCRIPTION: Heavy head with convex profile, short muscular neck, straight back and shoulders, sloping quarters, low-set tail and coarse upright mane

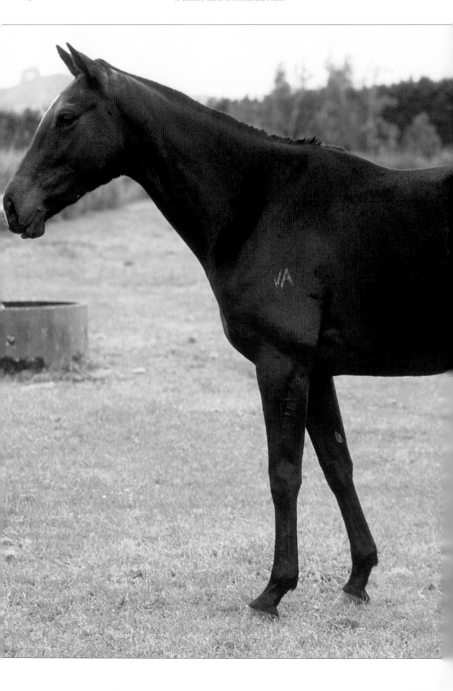

AUSTRALIAN STOCK HORSE

The Waler, the first Australian horse breed, had almost died out after the Second World War, some of the few remaining animals were crossed with Arabs and Thoroughbreds, and later with the American Quarter Horse. The result was the Australian Stock Horse, which was a versatile working horse suitable for every need. In looks it resembles the Thoroughbred, and has this breed's speed and good action, but the Waler gave it great stamina and endurance as well as an amiable temperament. The Australian Stock Horse Society was formed in 1971 and by 1979 had registered 40,000 horses. Today the Australian Stock Horse is not only used on farms but has also excelled at a variety of sports including dressage and show jumping – as well as the Australian sport of campdrafting, in which horse and rider separate a beast from a herd of cattle and work it round a course.

COUNTRY: Australia
BLOOD TEMPERATURE: Warm
HEIGHT: 14.2–16.2 hands
COLOUR: Usually bay, can be any solid colour
ENVIRONMENT: Temperate grassland
USES: Riding, dressage, jumping
TEMPERAMENT: Easy-going, willing
DESCRIPTION: Attractive head with broad forehead, sloping shoulders, deep chest, strong back, powerful muscular quarters, hard feet

BRUMBY

COUNTRY: Australia
BLOOD TEMPERATURE:
Warm
HEIGHT: 14–15 hands
COLOUR: All colours
ENVIRONMENT: Temperate
grassland
USES: Feral
TEMPERAMENT: Rebellious
and wilful
DESCRIPTION: Varies
considerably, but usually
heavy head, straight
shoulders, sloping
quarters, strong legs

The Brumby is not an indigenous wild horse – it is descended from the first horses brought to Australia and as such is a mixture of many different breeds. It therefore has no set characteristics, but it adapted rather too well to the harsh climate of Australia and at one time lived in large herds. These began to harm the natural flora and fauna, and also damage stock fences, overgraze pasture and foul water supplies. Seen as a pest, Brumbies were slaughtered in large numbers in the 1960s, which led to public outrage. Currently still roaming wild in some areas, the Brumby is usually not a good-looking horse – although occasionally a fine specimen does occur. The breed has poor value as a domestic horse, however, as it is cunning, rebellious and wilful. Humane culling now keeps numbers under control and improves the general health of the herd.

WALER

Horses arrived in Australia with the First Fleet in 1788, brought from South Africa. Later horses from Europe were also imported, including Thoroughbreds and Arabs. After surviving the gruelling journey – which was estimated to have taken at least 9 months – the horses had to cope with a strange and wild environment and travel huge distances across bushland so only the very toughest survived. The initial area for breeding was New South Wales on Australia's east coast, where the horses were used on the vast sheep stations, so the breed was known as the Waler. A superb riding horse with great endurance, the Waler soon became known as an excellent horse for the cavalry and many animals were exported to the British and Indian armies in India. Numbers were so depleted by the end of the Second World War that the Waler was in danger of extinction.

COUNTRY: Australia
BLOOD TEMPERATURE: Warm
HEIGHT: 15–16.2 hands
COLOUR: Bay, chestnut, black, brown and grey
ENVIRONMENT: Temperate grassland
USES: Riding, dressage, jumping
TEMPERAMENT: Easy-going, willing
DESCRIPTION: Attractive head, sloping shoulders, deep chest, strong back, powerful muscular quarters, hard feet

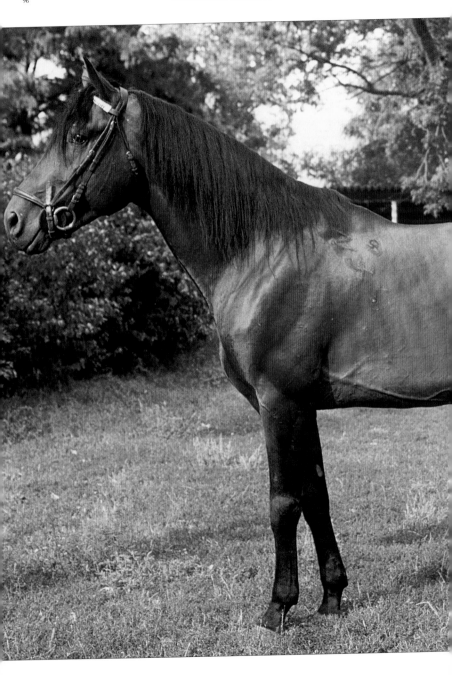

FURIOSO

Although it is now bred all over Central Europe, the Furioso was first developed at the Mezöhegyes stud in Hungary in the 19th century. Here a Thoroughbred stallion, Furioso, and later another stallion with some Norfolk Roadster blood, North Star, were crossed with Nonius mares. North Star had an illustrious pedigree, being the grandson of Touchstone, the 1834 winner of the St Leger and twice winner of the Ascot Gold Cup. The two bloodlines were originally kept separate, but after 1885 were bred together – which led to the Furioso characteristics becoming more prominent. An excellent competition horse, the Furioso is also very good in harness. The Thoroughbred blood gives the breed its good looks, speed and increased size, while the Nonius and Norfolk Roadster influence gives endurance, strength and hardiness. Although it is now comparatively rare worldwide, the Furioso is still very popular in some areas of Europe.

COUNTRY: Hungary
BLOOD TEMPERATURE: Warm
HEIGHT: 16 hands
COLOUR: Bay, chestnut, black
ENVIRONMENT: Cool temperate
USES: Riding, harness
TEMPERAMENT: Calm and adaptable
DESCRIPTION: Well-proportioned head, muscular neck with prolific mane, sloping shoulders, long back with muscular quarters, strong legs

GIDRAN ARABIAN

COUNTRY: Hungary
BLOOD TEMPERATURE: Hot
HEIGHT: Usually 16–16.2 hands, can be up to 17 hands
COLOUR: Usually chestnut
ENVIRONMENT: Temperate
USES: Riding, jumping
TEMPERAMENT: Can be temperamental
DESCRIPTION: Refined head, muscular well-proportioned body, sloping shoulders, deep chest, quite long back, muscular quarters, strong legs

Sometimes known as the Hungarian Anglo-Arab, the Gidran Arabian was first developed in the 19th century at the Mezőhegyes stud in Hungary. Initially the breed was meant to be a cavalry horse and several different breeds were used in the breeding programme, including the Transylvanian, Spanish, Nonius and local Hungarian, but finally the Thoroughbred and the Arab became the main bloodlines. Many horses were lost during the First World War, and afterwards the Arab and Kisber breeds were used to stabilize the remaining stock. The Gidran Arabian is known for its speed, agility, endurance and courage and is an excellent riding and jumping horse, as well as being very good in harness. It generally has a balanced temperament and is very elegant but powerful. The Gidran Arabian is currently an endangered breed since there are perhaps only around 200 in the world, mostly in Hungary.

NONIUS

This breed takes its name from the founding stallion, Nonius Senior, who foaled at Calvados in Normandy but was captured by the Hungarian cavalry in 1813 after the defeat of Napoleon at Leipzig. Nonius Senior was descended from an English half-bred and a Norman mare, but also had Norfolk Roadster blood; although not the most attractive horse, he was prolific and produced many excellent offspring. At the famous Mezőhegyes stud he was bred to a selection of mares of different breeds, including Andalusian, Arab, Kladruber and Lipizzaner and the resulting progeny were bred back to their sire. Two lines developed – a smaller one suitable for riding and a larger, heavier version for harness and light draught. Later English Thoroughbred stallions were used in the breeding programme to produce excellent competition horses. The Nonius is strong and well-built and although not particularly fast is an excellent all-round horse.

COUNTRY: Hungary
BLOOD TEMPERATURE: Warm
HEIGHT: 14.3–16.2 hands
COLOUR: Usually bay, sometimes chestnut or black
ENVIRONMENT: Cool temperate
USES: Riding, harness, light draught
TEMPERAMENT: Generally good natured
DESCRIPTION: Long head with a straight or convex profile, muscular arched neck, powerful shoulders, deep chest, wide back and quarters

SHAGYA ARABIAN

The Shagya Arabian was developed in the 19th century at the Bablona stud as the ultimate riding horse for the light cavalry of Hungary. Many oriental horses had arrived in Hungary in the 16–17th centuries, when the country was under Turkish occupation, so most Hungarian breeds have some Arab blood, but at Bablona they were concentrating on breeding a horse with all the Arab's good points but with a larger frame. The new breed took its name from its foundation sire, Shagya, who arrived at Bablona in 1836 from Syria, and combined the strength, endurance and looks of the Arab with additional height and strength. Many horses were lost in the 1940s and for a while the survival of the breed was in danger but it has now recovered. The Shagya Arabian is renowned for its speed and stamina and is a versatile horse, good in most competitive fields.

COUNTRY: Hungary
BLOOD TEMPERATURE: Hot
HEIGHT: Around 15.2 hands
COLOUR: Usually grey, can be any solid colour
ENVIRONMENT: Desert
COUNTRY: Hungary
USES: Riding, harness
TEMPERAMENT: Easy-going
DESCRIPTION: Attractive head with broad forehead, compact body, strong sloping shoulders, deep chest, muscular quarters, well-formed legs

LATVIAN

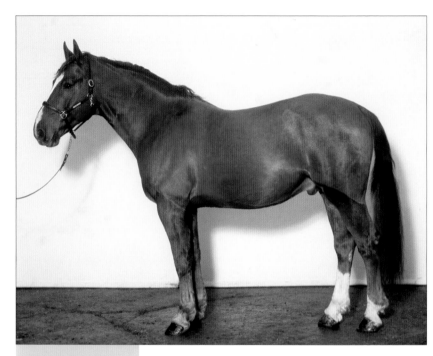

COUNTRY: Latvia
BLOOD TEMPERATURE: Warm
HEIGHT: 15–16 hands
COLOUR: Black, bay, brown, sometimes chestnut
ENVIRONMENT: Cool temperate
USES: Riding, harness, light draught
TEMPERAMENT: Calm and willing
DESCRIPTION: Rather large head on an elegant muscular neck, powerful sloping shoulders, broad chest, straight back, muscular quarters, strong legs

After the First World War there was a shortage of horses in Latvia so breeds such as the Oldenburg, Hanoverian and Holstein were imported to breed with local stock – which were probably descendants of the extinct Tarpan. Two types of Latvian horse were developed: a draught horse and a lighter version for riding. After Latvia became part of the Soviet Union, horse breeding was discouraged and private ownership was banned – all horses were the property of the state. Despite this, breeders continued to develop the bloodline, although outside the country the horses were not specifically designated as Latvian. After Latvia became independent again, in 1991, many stud farms were renewed; Latvian horses became better known and were increasingly bred for competition purposes. The renowned dressage horse Rusty, ridden by Ulla Salzgeber, is a Latvian and the breed is also an excellent and powerful jumper.

KABARDIN

A mountain horse, the Kabardin was developed by the mountain people of the North Caucasus during the 16th century and includes Turkoman, Arab and Persian blood and that of local steppe horses. However, the biggest influence on the breed's development has been its environment – the treacherous mountain terrain has made it surefooted, while the harsh weather of the region gave it extraordinary stamina and endurance. The Kabardin also developed a useful homing ability, and is able to find its way in darkness or misty conditions. During the Russian Revolution and the Second World War numbers fell drastically, but later efforts were made to re-establish the breed. Today the Kabardin is known as frugal to keep, long-lived and enduring and is in demand as an excellent riding horse – some are natural pacers. It is also suitable for harness work and is noted for its endurance over long distances.

COUNTRY: North Caucasus
BLOOD temperature: Warm
HEIGHT: 15–15.2 hands
COLOUR: Bay, brown or black
ENVIRONMENT: Mountain
USES: Riding, trekking, harness
TEMPERAMENT: Even-tempered, willing
DESCRIPTION: Attractive head, often with Roman nose, short muscular neck, straight powerful shoulders, straight back, short strong legs, hard hooves

TERSK

COUNTRY: North Caucasus
BLOOD TEMPERATURE: Warm
HEIGHT: 14.3–15.2 hands
COLOUR: Gray, sometimes chestnut
ENVIRONMENT: Steppes
USES: Riding, jumping
TEMPERAMENT: Willing, gentle and intelligent
DESCRIPTION: Attractive head on a well-formed muscular neck, sloping shoulders, broad deep chest, straight back with muscular quarters, muscular legs

A relatively new breed, the Tersk was only developed in the early 20th century at the Tersk and Stavropol studs of Soviet Russia. It was intended as a re-creation of the Strelets Arab, which had been very popular with the army and as a result had almost been wiped out during the Russian Revolution. Only a few purebred horses were left, so Don, Kabardin and Arabian horses were used in the breeding programme and by 1948 the new breed was officially recognized as the Tersk. At the studs, the horses are currently kept in large herds on the open steppes, but their diet and condition is carefully monitored at all times. An extremely tough horse, the Tersk is also very attractive and athletic and has the Arab's spectacular and graceful movement. It is an excellent mount for endurance rides and is also suitable for show jumping and eventing – as well as being fast enough for racing.

TRAKEHNER

A particularly fine and elegant horse, the Trakehner originated in the 13th century in what was once East Prussia. The base stock was descended from the Tarpan, but in 1732 King Friedrich Wilhelm I founded a stud at Trakehner to develop coach horses and later a cavalry horse for his army. The emphasis was on creating a horse that was fast, sound and tough, but which also looked elegant and attractive. The breeding programme first used Arab, Turkoman and Thoroughbred horses, but since the stud book was established in 1877 outside blood has only been permitted under strict control. During the Second World War many of the best horses fell into Russian hands, and only around 100 survived the trek west to escape. These horses later formed the nucleus to rebuild the breed. Today the Trakehner is recognized as an excellent horse in almost every area of competition, appearing at the highest levels.

COUNTRY: Poland
BLOOD TEMPERATURE: Warm
HEIGHT: 16–17 hands
COLOUR: All solid colours
ENVIRONMENT: Cool temperate
USES: Riding, dressage, jumping
TEMPERAMENT: Quiet, easy-going, energetic
DESCRIPTION: Finely modelled head on an elegant neck, powerful sloping shoulders, deep wide chest, compact back, powerful quarters, high-set tail

WIELKOPOLSKI

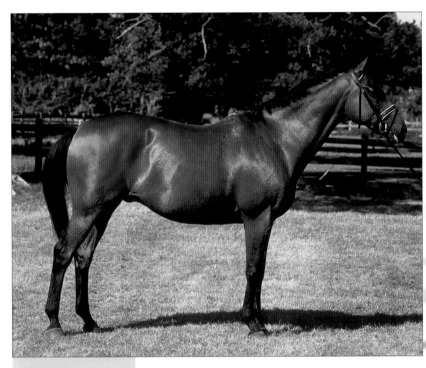

COUNTRY: Poland
BLOOD TEMPERATURE: Warm
HEIGHT: 16–16.2 hands
COLOUR: All solid colours
ENVIRONMENT: Cool temperate
USES: Riding, dressage, harness
TEMPERAMENT: Easy-going
DESCRIPTION: Fine head with a straight profile, long elegant neck, sloping muscular shoulders, deep wide chest, compact body, powerful quarters, long legs

The Wielkopolski is a new breed that was only developed in the mid-20th century by crossbreeding the Masuren and Poznan – both of which are now officially extinct. The Masuren was very similar to the Trakehner and the Poznan was a blend of Arab, Thoroughbred and Hanoverian. The Wielkopolski was specifically bred as a riding and driving horse and is strong, hardy, athletic and fast. It is very good-looking and is valued for its paces, which include a long, free walk and a comfortable level trot, as well as a fast canter and gallop that can easily cover considerable ground. The breed is often used for carriage driving – particularly in competition – but is also excellent for dressage, as well as for jumping and eventing. The Wielkopolski is very popular in Poland and surrounding areas of Europe, but is less well-known worldwide.

RUSSIAN TROTTER

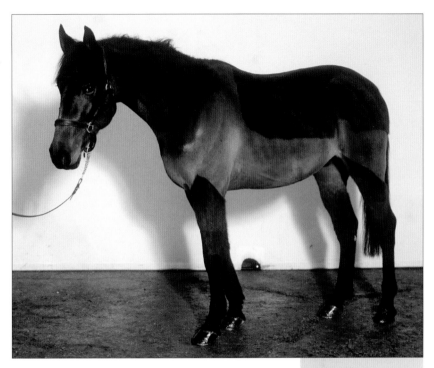

For many years the Orlov Trotter was unsurpassed for racing in Europe, but at the end of the 19th century the American Standardbred arrived in Russia and proved to be faster than the Orlov. It was decided to crossbreed the two to improve the Orlov's speed, but although the new horse was indeed very much faster it did not have the Orlov's beauty, power or stamina. Although some felt that the Orlov bloodline was being contaminated, others felt that looks were less important than speed so the Russian Trotter was recognized as a new breed in 1949. Since then studs have been selectively breeding to improve its conformation, while purebred Orlov blood or Standardbred blood is still added as required to maintain the characteristics of the breed. The Russian Trotter has an excellent temperament, being energetic but easy to train.

COUNTRY: Russia
BLOOD TEMPERATURE: Warm
HEIGHT: 15.3–16 hands
COLOUR: Bay, sometimes black, chestnut or grey
ENVIRONMENT: Taiga
USES: Harness
TEMPERAMENT: Generally good
DESCRIPTION: Plain well-set head on a long muscular neck, wide deep chest, long sloping muscular shoulders, long back, strong legs

BUDYONNY

COUNTRY: Russia
BLOOD TEMPERATURE: Warm
HEIGHT: Up to 16 hands
COLOUR: Mostly chestnut, can be any solid colour
ENVIRONMENT: Temperate
USES: Riding
TEMPERAMENT: Easy-going, energetic
DESCRIPTION: Attractive head on a well-formed neck, straight back with sloping shoulders and quarters, wide deep chest, strong legs, well-set tail

In 1921, just after the Russian Revolution, the Soviet Union began to breed a new cavalry horse that was later named after the Russian cavalry hero Marshall Budyonny. The base stock included Russian Chernomor and Don mares crossed with English Thoroughbred stallions, and initially the breed was known as the Anglo-Don. More Thoroughbred blood was added later, as necessary. A stud book was first published in 1934 and the breed has been officially recognized since 1948. The Budyonny is usually chestnut, often with a wonderful metallic sheen. The breed has a calm and quiet temperament, but can be energetic, lively and tough. It is an excellent all-round sporting horse, with formidable endurance, a good gallop, and an athletic jump. It is often used in endurance competitions, as well as for steeplechasing, jumping and dressage.

DON

Named after the river that flows across the Russian steppes, the Don evolved in the 18th and 19th centuries – originally as a mount for Cossack cavalry. A mixture of Mongolian, Turkoman, Karabakh, Akhal-Teke, Arab, Orlov and Thoroughbred blood, the Don is fast, tough and adaptable, but can be rather unprepossessing in appearance. Its straight shoulders give it a rather choppy and uncomfortable action, but its endurance and ability to cope with extreme hardship make it useful for long-distance events and it is also popular in harness. It is often used in the tourist industry, pulling the traditional tachanka harnessed four abreast. The Don was almost wiped out during the First World War and the Revolution at the beginning of the 20th century, but was later used to develop other breeds – such as the Budyonny – and has recently been enjoying a revival.

COUNTRY: Russia
BLOOD TEMPERATURE: Warm
HEIGHT: 15.2–16.2 hands
COLOUR: Chestnut, bay, sometimes grey
ENVIRONMENT: Steppes
USES: Riding, harness
TEMPERAMENT: Good-natured
DESCRIPTION: Average-size head on a well-formed muscular neck, upright shoulders, deep broad chest, long straight back, often weak quarters and low-set tail

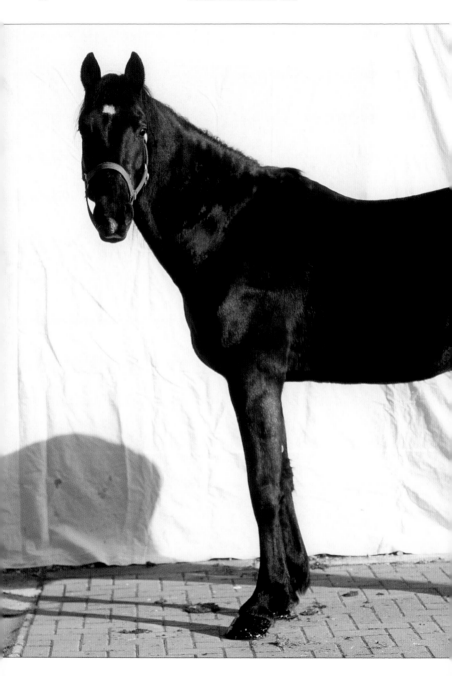

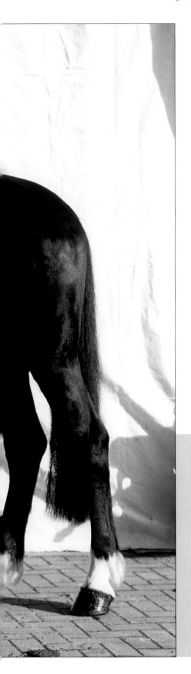

ORLOV TROTTER

The Orlov Trotter was first developed by Count Alexei Orlov in the 18th century at his stud in Khrenov in central Russia. The breed was based on Arab stallions crossed with Spanish and Danish mares, as well as English Thoroughbreds and Dutch Friesians, with the best progeny interbred to establish fixed characteristics. The foundation stallion was Bars I, foaled in 1784, the grandson of a white Arab, Smetanka. The Orlov Trotter was intended to be fast and enduring, to be used as both a fast and attractive carriage horse and a racing trotting horse. Later crossbreeding with the American Standardbred produced the Russian Trotter, which was much faster but lacked the Orlov's refinement and often had conformational defects. The Orlov Trotter is a lightweight horse, but has great stamina and endurance and is widely used in trotting races in Russia.

COUNTRY: Russia
BLOOD TEMPERATURE: Warm
HEIGHT: 15.2–17 hands
COLOUR: Grey, black, bay
ENVIRONMENT: Taiga
USES: Harness
TEMPERAMENT: Generally good
DESCRIPTION: Fine head on an arched neck set high, straight shoulders, deep girth, long straight back with powerful quarters, long legs

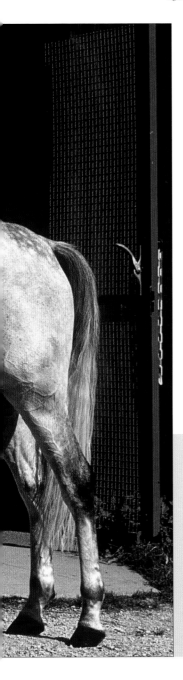

ARAB

One of the oldest purebred horses in the world, the Arab has been documented in drawings dating from long before the Christian era – although few hard facts about its exact origins are available. It has been used as the foundation for many other breeds, including the English Thoroughbred. The absence of any external bloodlines has meant that the Arab has retained its distinct characteristics, including its unique build and high tail carriage that comes from having 17 ribs, 5 lumbar vertebrae and 16 tail bones, unlike almost all other breeds which have 18:6:18. The Arab also has a distinctive shield-shaped bulge on its forehead, known as the jibbah. The Arab is now bred all around the world, with each country having its own stud book, although these are all ultimately approved by the World Arab Horse Organization in the interests of breed harmony.

COUNTRY: Arabian peninsula
BLOOD TEMPERATURE: Hot
HEIGHT: Up to 15 hands
COLOUR: All solid colours
ENVIRONMENT: Desert
USES: Riding
TEMPERAMENT: Sociable, good tempered
DESCRIPTION: Small refined head with dished profile and tapering muzzle, elegant arched neck, deep broad chest, strong back, broad quarters, high-set tail

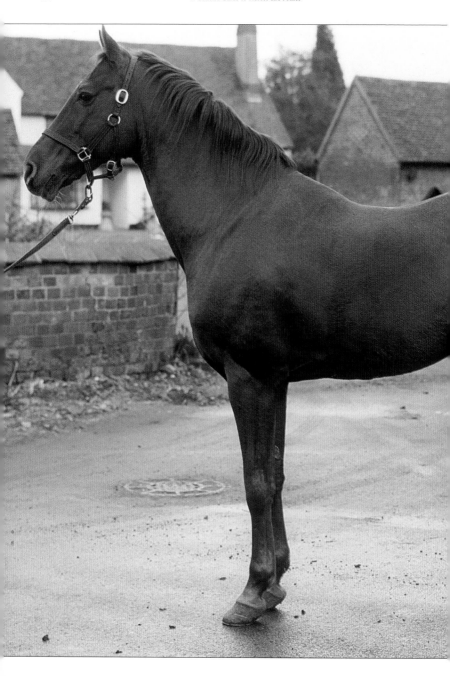

PERSIAN ARAB

The name Persian Arab is a general one that covers several different lines found across Iran, each of which has a specific name from the family that bred it. Although very similar to the Arab, the Persian Arab is a slightly heavier horse but is still a very attractive animal with natural bearing. Like the Arab it is fast and agile, with great stamina and enormous spirit, and is now used mainly for racing – although before the motor vehicle it was valued as the only means of transport. The Persian Arab is believed to have existed even as far back as 2000 BC, so it is one of the world's oldest breeds. Many horses were wiped out in the mid-20th century, when African horse sickness spread across Iran, and now breeding is strictly controlled to preserve the pure strains that currently exist.

COUNTRY: Iran
BLOOD TEMPERATURE: Hot
HEIGHT: 14.2–15.2 hands
COLOUR: Grey, bay, chestnut
ENVIRONMENT: Desert
USES: Riding
TEMPERAMENT: Sociable, good tempered
DESCRIPTION: Refined head with dished profile and tapering muzzle, arched neck, deep broad chest, compact muscular back, rounded quarters, high-set tail

CANADIAN CUTTING HORSE

COUNTRY: Canada
BLOOD TEMPERATURE: Warm
HEIGHT: Up to 16 hands
COLOUR: All solid colours
ENVIRONMENT: Cool temperate
USES: Riding, agriculture
TEMPERAMENT: Easy-going, sociable
DESCRIPTION: Well-proportioned head, muscular well-set neck, powerful sloping shoulders, broad deep chest, straight back, powerful muscular quarters, short strong legs

As its name suggests, the Canadian Cutting Horse was developed in Canada specifically for working cows on the ranch. It is very similar to the American Quarter Horse, on which it is based, and like this breed it also has elements of Spanish blood – since Spanish horses are renowned for their ability to work cattle. In ranching it is often necessary to remove one cow from the herd for treatment or branding and this is much easier with a specially trained horse, which can out-think and out-manoeuvre the cow. The Canadian Cutting Horse is quick, intelligent, calm and willing and also very agile, able to turn sharply at top speed. As well as ranch work the breed also appears in the very popular cutting shows, where as many selected cows as possible are removed from the herd within a time limit and rewards for the best performance can be very high.

AMERICAN BASHKIR CURLY

The exact origin of the American Bashkir Curly is one of the mysteries of the horse world; a herd was discovered in 1898 in central Nevada, but curly coated horses are mentioned in American Indian pictograms dating back to the early 1800s. It was once thought that these horses were descended from Russian Bashkir Curlies that had been abandoned by Russian settlers in the Northwest Territories in the 1700s – hence the American breed's name – but it has since been proved that the two breeds are not related. The American Bashkir Curly Registry was established in 1971 to promote the breed, which is becoming increasingly popular. The unusual curly coat is often shed in summer and regrown in winter, when it can range from soft waves like crushed velvet to tight curls. The double mane falls on either side of the neck in tight ringlets.

COUNTRY: United States
BLOOD TEMPERATURE: Warm
HEIGHT: 14.3–15 hands
COLOUR: All colours
ENVIRONMENT: Mountain
USES: Riding, agriculture
Temperament: Calm and gentle
DESCRIPTION: Curly coat, heavy head with wide forehead, short muscular neck, stout but well-proportioned body

APPALOOSA

For centuries spotted horses were shown in Chinese and Asian art, but there are two theories on how they arrived in North America. One holds that they were brought in the 16th century by the Spanish and acquired by Plains Indians – specifically the Nez Perce tribe, who were renowned for their horse breeding skills. Another theory holds that the spotted horse travelled across a land bridge from Asia with northwest Indian tribes at the end of the last ice age. Whichever is true, the Nez Perce were proud of their distinctive horses – the spotted coat offered excellent camouflage and the breed is fast and athletic, with plenty of stamina. There are five patterns: blanket, white over the hips with or without spots; marble, dark colouring on the edges and a frost pattern in the middle; leopard, white with dark spots; snowflake, heavy spotting on the hips; and frost, white speckles on a dark ground. The name Appaloosa was officially adopted only in 1938 when a breed society was formed.

COUNTRY: United States
BLOOD TEMPERATURE: Warm
HEIGHT: 14.2–15.2 hands
COLOUR: Spotted
ENVIRONMENT: Temperate grassland
USES: Riding
TEMPERAMENT: Good natured and sociable
DESCRIPTION: Spotted coat, small head with straight profile, long muscular neck, deep chest, sloping shoulders, short compact back, rounded muscular quarters

AMERICAN SADDLEBRED

COUNTRY: United States
BLOOD TEMPERATURE:
  Warm
HEIGHT: 15–16 hands
COLOUR: All solid colours
ENVIRONMENT: Cool
  temperate
USES: Riding, harness
TEMPERAMENT: Generally
  good but spirited
DESCRIPTION: Quality head
  on a muscular neck set
  high on the shoulders,
  broad chest, level croup,
  high-set tail, long
  elegant legs

The American Saddlebred was once called the Kentucky
Saddler and originated in Kentucky in the 19th century,
where it was developed as an all-round breed. Based on
the now extinct Narragansett Pacer and the Canadian
Pacer – both of which were naturally gaited – the
American Saddlebred also had Morgan and
Thoroughbred blood to give it eye-catching good looks
and impressive speed. It is now mainly used in the show
ring, where three-gaited horses perform the walk, trot
and canter with an exaggerated and flashy action. Five-
gaited horses also exhibit a prancing four-beat slow gait
and an extremely impressive full speed ahead action
known as the 'rack'. For show purposes the feet are
grown long and shod with special heavy shoes, but if the
hooves are trimmed normally the American Saddlebred
makes a versatile mount for all types of riding.

COLORADO RANGER

The Colorado Ranger, also known as the Rangerbred, has a well documented history. It dates back to 1878 when General Ulysses S. Grant was given an Arab stallion, Leopard, and a Barb stallion, Linden Trees by Turkish Sultan Abdul Hamid II, which were bred to local mares. The foals were excellent workers, and the new breed became known as the Colorado Ranger. Later two spotted stallions were used in the breeding programme and many Colorado Rangers now have spotted coats – although the essential factors to the breed registry are conformation and pedigree, not colour. The only outside blood now permitted is Thoroughbred, Quarter Horse, Arab, Appaloosa or Lusitano. The Colorado Ranger is a first class riding horse with an excellent disposition, but is not well known because until 1968 registration in the breed association was limited to 50 people.

COUNTRY: United States
BLOOD TEMPERATURE: Warm
HEIGHT: Up to 16 hands
COLOUR: Any colour, often spotted
ENVIRONMENT: Temperate grassland
USES: Riding
TEMPERAMENT: Easy-going, sociable
DESCRIPTION: Attractive head on a long muscular neck, deep wide chest, rounded barrel and compact back, powerful hindquarters

MISSOURI FOX TROTTER

Developed in the Ozarks in the early 19th century by settlers, the Missouri Fox Trotter was intended as a general all-rounder suitable to cover long distances comfortably. It was based on crossing Morgan and Thoroughbred stock, with later infusions of Spanish blood as well as Tennessee Walking Horse and Saddlebred. The Missouri Fox Trotter is famous for its sliding fox trot gait, in which it apparently walks fast with its front legs with the hind legs trotting – an very smooth, swinging action that produces a speed of up to 10 mph (16 km/h) over short distances but can also be maintained for long distances. It also has a long, easy-going, four-beat walk – known as a flat foot walk – and a 'rocking horse' canter. As well as ranch work, the Missouri Fox Trotter is popular for endurance riding, trekking and for showing.

COUNTRY: United States
BLOOD TEMPERATURE: Warm
HEIGHT: 14–16 hands
COLOUR: Mostly chestnut, but can be any solid colour
ENVIRONMENT: Cool temperate
USES: Riding
TEMPERAMENT: Easy-going, amenable
DESCRIPTION: Well-proportioned head with straight profile, muscular neck set into sloping shoulders, compact back, muscular powerful quarters

MORAB

COUNTRY: United States
BLOOD TEMPERATURE: Warm
HEIGHT: 14.1–16.1 hands
COLOUR: All solid colours
ENVIRONMENT: Cool temperate
USES: Riding
TEMPERAMENT: Easy-going, calm, friendly
DESCRIPTION: Fine head with straight or concave profile, muscular neck, nicely sloping shoulders, deep chest, compact back, muscular quarters with high-set tail

Based on a cross between an Arab and a Morgan, the Morab was first developed in the American west in the early 1800s as an all-round working horse; although other Arab crosses were also tried, the Arab-Morgan was the most successful. In the 1920s publisher William Randolph Hearst had both an Arab and Morab breeding programme and he is credited with coining the Morab name. Like the Arab, the Morab has 17 ribs, 5 lumbar vertebrae and 16 tail bones and the breed also has the Arab's looks and refinement and the Morgan's strength, speed and endurance. It is a naturally athletic breed and is valued for jumping and dressage, but also excels at cutting. The Morab is also very intelligent, dependable and affectionate, so it is an ideal mount for children, novices and senior riders.

MORGAN

The Morgan is an unusual breed in that it can be traced back to a single stallion, Figure, a small bay given to a man named Justin Morgan in the 1790s. The stallion's exact breeding was unknown, but Thoroughbred, Welsh Cob and Arab blood are all believed to have been involved. Since he stood only around 14 hands not much was expected of Figure, but he proved to be exceptionally hardworking and was unbeaten in saddle and harness races and at weight pulling competitions. He was also intelligent, handsome and spirited and soon became well known as the 'Justin Morgan' horse – a name that became his own after his owner died. The stallion passed on his talents to all his progeny, which became known as the Morgan breed. The Morgan is now widely used both for leisure riding and for showing.

COUNTRY: United States
BLOOD TEMPERATURE: Warm
HEIGHT: 14.2–15.2 hands
COLOUR: All solid colours, rarely grey
ENVIRONMENT: Temperate
USES: Riding, harness
TEMPERAMENT: Calm, intelligent
DESCRIPTION: Attractive head set on an arched muscular neck, powerful shoulders and broad chest, wide short back, rounded quarters and well-set tail

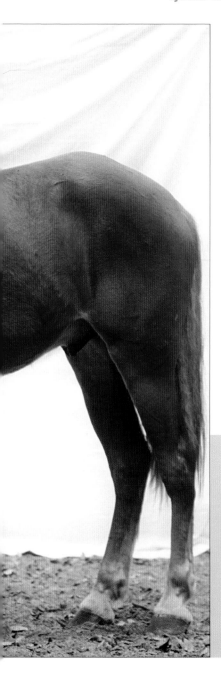

MUSTANG

A feral horse, the Mustang was originally descended from the Spanish horses brought to America by the conquistadors, which had escaped or been set free to form wild herds. Later these herds were augmented with horses released by Native American tribes or ranchers and by cavalry horses that had escaped from battle, so the Mustang can be a mix of several different breeds. The herds grew rapidly and by the beginning of the 20th century were widely regarded as a nuisance, so ranchers often shot them or they were killed for meat or pet food. By 1970 the herds were vastly reduced and since 1971 these wild horses have been protected by law. Mustangs are generally hardy, fast and agile, although unchecked breeding means they can degenerate into poor quality stock. They can be tamed and often make ideal ranch horses.

COUNTRY: United States
BLOOD TEMPERATURE: Warm
HEIGHT: 13–15 hands
COLOUR: All colours
ENVIRONMENT: Savannah
USES: Feral
TEMPERAMENT: Often rebellious, temperamental
DESCRIPTION: Wide variance due to their feral nature, but often have a Spanish-type head and Roman nose, short back and strong legs

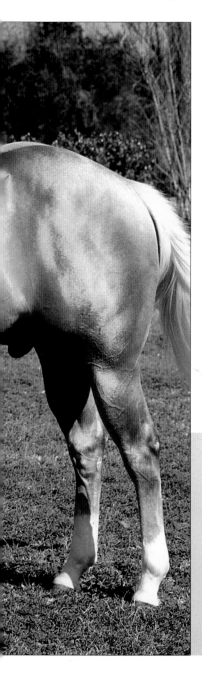

PALOMINO

Strictly speaking the Palomino is a colour and not a breed, but associations in both the United States and Britain register horses that meet specific requirements and some are lobbying for it to be recognized as a breed. The origins of the Palomino are unknown, but golden horses are found throughout history and feature in several famous works of art. A Palomino can be created from many other breeds — what is important is the coat colour, and the favoured cross to achieve the required coloration is either a chestnut-palomino, or a chestnut with a cream or albino — crossing a palomino to a palomino usually gives a cremello, which looks like an albino. The main coat colour should be either the colour of a newly minted gold coin, or up to three shades lighter or darker, and although white markings are accepted on the legs they should not extend above the hock. The mane and tail should be silvery white.

COUNTRY: United States
BLOOD TEMPERATURE: Warm
HEIGHT: Up to 17 hands
COLOUR: Gold with white mane and tail
ENVIRONMENT: Temperate
USES: Riding
TEMPERAMENT: Generally easy-going
DESCRIPTION: Varies, but tend to have an attractive head, well-formed neck, reasonably sloping shoulders, straight back and muscular quarters

PINTO

The Pinto and the related Paint Horse are only considered to be breeds in North America; elsewhere they are considered to be coat colours as what is important is the horse's coloration. The Pinto can be of any breeding but must have one of two patterns: Tobiano, in which the coat appears to be white with large flowing spots of colour, or Overo, in which the coat appears to be coloured with large areas of white. The Paint horse has the same colorations but is restricted to horses of documented Paint, Quarter Horse or Thoroughbred breeding. The colouring of these horses is called piebald – for black and white – or skewbald – for any other colour and white – in the United Kingdom. These horses were particularly prized in North American Indian culture but are now generally popular as riding horses.

COUNTRY: United States
BLOOD TEMPERATURE: Warm
HEIGHT: Up to 16 hands
COLOUR: Any colour plus white
ENVIRONMENT: Savannah
USES: Riding
TEMPERAMENT: Generally good natured
DESCRIPTION: Two-colour coat, varies in conformation but generally quality head, muscular shoulders and quarters, compact back

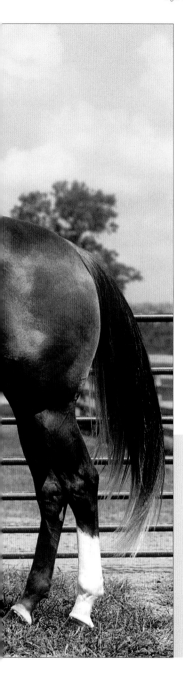

QUARTER HORSE

The first all-American breed, the Quarter Horse is perhaps the most popular breed in the world. It was first developed in the 17th century when Thoroughbreds brought by the English were crossed with Andalusian, Barb and Arab horses brought by the Spanish conquistadors beforehand. The 'quarter' in the breed's name comes from the English habit of racing these horses over a quarter of a mile – the breed is explosively fast over short distances and the powerful quarters allow it to sprint from a standing start. After distance racing became popular the Quarter Horse could not compete against the Thoroughbred, but it soon became apparent that it was an exceptional ranch animal with great ability to work cows. The Quarter Horse also has a wonderful temperament and makes an excellent workhorse, which makes it suitable for all kinds of riding as well as jobs around the farm.

COUNTRY: United States
BLOOD TEMPERATURE: Warm
HEIGHT: 14–16 hands
COLOUR: All solid colours
ENVIRONMENT: Cool temperate
USES: Riding
TEMPERAMENT: Good natured and calm
DESCRIPTION: Short head with broad forehead, muscular well-formed neck, wide deep chest, strong sloping shoulders, compact body, strong quarters

ROCKY MOUNTAIN

COUNTRY: United States
BLOOD TEMPERATURE: Warm
HEIGHT: Up to 16 hands
COLOUR: All solid colours, no white on body
ENVIRONMENT: Temperate mountains
USES: Riding, trekking, harness
TEMPERAMENT: Easy-going, kind
DESCRIPTION: Intelligent head on a long graceful neck, deep wide neck, muscular shoulders, well-proportioned back

The Rocky Mountain horse is a larger version of the Rocky Mountain pony, measuring up to 16 hands. Like the pony, it was developed in the late 1980s by Sam Tuttle of Stout Springs in Kentucky, who ran riding tours into the Natural Bridge State Park. He discovered that all riders seemed to be comfortable on his stallion Old Tobe, with his surefooted, four-beat gait. He bred a line of horses and ponies from Old Tobe, who inherited his gait and were also sturdy, robust and had his calm and amiable nature. The Rocky Mountain has a great deal of stamina and can cover long distances over rough terrain. It is not only popular with riders, but can also be used in light harness to pull buggies and carriages. Although the Rocky Mountain comes in many colours, the most prized is a deep chocolate with a flaxen mane and tail.

STANDARDBRED

The supreme harness racer, the Standardbred was based on an English Thoroughbred, Messenger, with Norfolk Trotter blood, with later infusions from the Narragansett Pacer and the Morgan. The foundation sire was one of Messenger's offspring, Hambletonian 10, foaled in 1849. Although the Standardbred was developed for its speed – it is the fastest harness racer in the world – it retains some of its Thoroughbred ancestor's looks. It can either trot normally with the legs moving in diagonal pairs, or pace with the legs on each side trotting together – pacers are generally preferred in the United States, trotters in Europe. The fastest time recorded for a trotter is 1 mile (1.6 km) in 1 minute 55.25 seconds, and for a pacer 1 mile (1.6 km) in 1 minute 52 seconds – which is equivalent to 32mph (51.2 km/h). The breed is very competitive and loves to race.

COUNTRY: United States
BLOOD TEMPERATURE: Warm
HEIGHT: 14–16 hands
COLOUR: All solid colours
ENVIRONMENT: Cool temperate
USES: Harness
TEMPERAMENT: Generally good
DESCRIPTION: Refined head on a medium-length neck, long back, powerful quarters, croup usually higher than withers, good legs

TENNESSEE WALKING HORSE

The Tennessee Walking Horse was developed in the 19th century as a general purpose animal that would be suitable for riding, driving in harness and working on the land. It was based on the now extinct Narragansett Pacer, but also includes Thoroughbred, Morgan, Standardbred and Saddlebred blood. The breed has three natural gaits: a flat-foot walk, which is smooth and even; a unique four-beat running walk that can achieve a speed of 8 mph (12.8 km/h); and a smooth, rolling canter. The breed registry was founded in 1935 and was closed in 1948 – from then on, only horses with parents already registered could be registered themselves. Originally ridden by plantation owners, doctors and country preachers – all of whom spent a great deal of time in the saddle – the Tennessee Walking Horse is now a popular mount for all the family.

COUNTRY: United States
USES: Riding
BLOOD TEMPERATURE: Warm
HEIGHT: 13.2–17.1 hands
COLOUR: All colours
ENVIRONMENT: Cool temperate
TEMPERAMENT: Very calm, easy-going
DESCRIPTION: Large head with a straight profile, muscular arched neck, sloping shoulders, broad chest, short back and high-set tail

BELGIAN WARMBLOOD

COUNTRY: Belgium
BLOOD TEMPERATURE: Warm
HEIGHT: Up to 16.2 hands
COLOUR: All solid colours, mostly bay
ENVIRONMENT: Cool temperate
USES: Riding
TEMPERAMENT: Calm, easy-going
DESCRIPTION: Attractive head on a well-set muscular neck, broad chest, sloping shoulders, compact back, muscular quarters, strong legs

One of the newest warmbloods, the Belgian Warmblood was specifically developed as a competition horse in the Brabant area of Belgium and it excels at both dressage and jumping. In the mid 20th century, lighter examples of the local farm horses were bred to Gelderlanders, which produced a heavier riding horse, and later Selle Français was added for improved looks, and Holstein and Havoverian blood for agility. Finally Thoroughbred, Anglo-Arab and Dutch Warmblood were used in the breeding programme, which resulted in today's excellent all-round competition horse. The Belgian Warmblood is a powerful and reliable horse, with a calm temperament and has become increasingly popular in Europe and the United States. The studbook is carefully monitored to ensure that its required qualities are maintained, with each individual horse going through an approval system before it is accepted.

CLEVELAND BAY

The Cleveland Bay dates back to the Middle Ages, when it developed in the Cleveland area of Yorkshire in Britain. A local strain of bay coloured horses, the Chapman, had great pulling power and no leg feathering – an advantage on the local clay soils – and these were mated with Barb and Spanish horses in the 17th century. In the 18th century Thoroughbred blood was introduced to produce the Yorkshire Coach Horse, which was much faster, and the Cleveland Bay fell out of favour. By 1962 it was almost extinct, when Queen Elizabeth II purchased one of the remaining four stallions, Mulgrave Supreme, and sent him to stud. The Cleveland Bay is now used to pull royal coaches on ceremonial occasions and the breed is enjoying a revival, although still endangered. As well as coach horses, they are excellent competition horses, either purebred or crossed with Thoroughbreds.

COUNTRY: Britain
BLOOD temperature: Warm
HEIGHT: 16–16.2 hands
COLOUR: Bay
ENVIRONMENT: Cool temperate
USES: Riding, harness
TEMPERAMENT: Good natured and calm
DESCRIPTION: Large head on a muscular arched neck, strong muscular shoulders and chest, straight back, powerful quarters, short clean legs

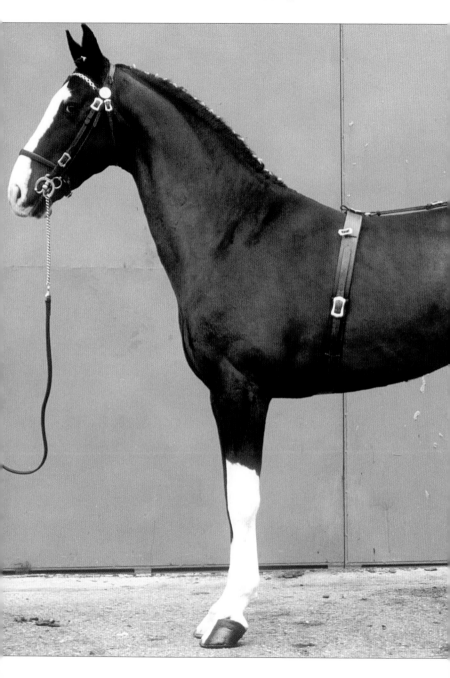

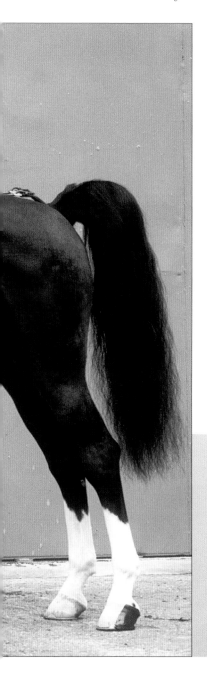

HACKNEY HORSE

The word 'hackney' probably comes from the French word haquenée, which means an all-purpose horse or nag, and from medieval times a hackney was the general name for a riding horse of particular stamina. In the early 18th century Arab blood was added to the line and the Hackney was prized for its ability to cover long distances at an even trot, when the major form of transport was by horse-drawn carriage. After the Second World War, when motorised transport became more widespread the role of the Hackney was threatened, but breeders then began to concentrate on developing a show horse. Today's Hackney Horse is a spectacular performer in the show ring, and also takes part in driving competitions at international level. It has a stylish floating action and great stamina, as well as being both athletic and elegant.

COUNTRY: Britain
BLOOD TEMPERATURE: Warm
HEIGHT: 14–15.3 hands
COLOUR: All solid colours
ENVIRONMENT: Cool temperate
USES: Harness
TEMPERAMENT: Generally easy-going, can be temperamental
DESCRIPTION: Small head with a slightly convex profile, long graceful neck, powerful low-set shoulders, compact body, high-set tail

THOROUGHBRED

Developed in Britain in the 17th and 18th centuries, the Thoroughbred is renowned worldwide and every horse in the stud book can trace its ancestry back to one of three sires. The Bylerley Turk was captured from the Turks in battle in 1689 and despite the name was probably an Arab or an Akhal-Teke; his grandson, Herod, was founder of one of the four principal Thoroughbred lines and Herod's son, Highflyer, was founder of another. The Darley Arabian was bought in Syria in 1704 and put to stud in Yorkshire; his great-grandson, Eclipse – a famous racehorse, unbeaten during his career – became founder of another Thoroughbred line. Finally the Godolphin Arabian, a Barb not an Arabian, came to Britain in 1728 and was initially used as a 'teaser' to test mares for other stallions. His grandson, Matchem, foaled in 1748, was founder of the fourth Thoroughbred line. The Thoroughbred has almost perfect proportions and is the fastest horse in the world, able to reach 45 mph (72 km/h) and jump to 10 m (30 ft).

COUNTRY: Britain
BLOOD TEMPERATURE: Hot
HEIGHT: 16–16.2 hands
COLOUR: All solid colours
ENVIRONMENT: Cool temperate
USES: Riding
TEMPERAMENT: Highly strung
DESCRIPTION: Finely-modelled head on an elegant arched neck, sloping shoulders, short strong back, powerful muscular quarters, long legs

ANGLO-ARAB

Created by crossing the Arab with the Thoroughbred, the Anglo-Arab was first developed in Britain in the 18th and 19th centuries, but the breed was perfected in France from the 19th century onwards. The aim was to create a horse that had the best qualities of both breeds – the endurance, stamina and good nature of the Arab and the strength and speed of the Thoroughbred without its excitable temperament. The science of breeding a good Anglo-Arab is quite exact – 50 per cent pairings can result in an offspring that is slower than its parents, but the standard requires no less than 25 per cent Arab blood and no more than 75 per cent. The Anglo-Arab is a natural athlete and is fast and able to jump well, which makes it ideal for eventing, but it is also very easy to train, which makes it good for both dressage and show jumping.

COUNTRY: Britain & France
BLOOD TEMPERATURE: Hot
HEIGHT: 15.2–16.2 hands
COLOUR: Mostly bay or chestnut, can be any solid colour
ENVIRONMENT: Cool temperate
USES: Riding, dressage
TEMPERAMENT: Generally good natured, can be a little temperamental
DESCRIPTION: Finely-modelled head with straight profile, long sloping neck, powerful sloping shoulders, compact body with deep chest, well-muscled quarters, long slender legs

WELSH COB

The Welsh Cob is a larger version of the Welsh Mountain Pony, with a high stepping, showy trot that possibly comes from the Norfolk Trotter and Yorkshire Coach Horse blood that was introduced in the 18th and 19th centuries. Arab blood was also used in the breeding programme, which has given the Welsh Cob its attractive looks. A versatile horse with plenty of stamina, it has been used on local farms, to pull heavy artillery equipment and as a mount for cavalry regiments of the army, and to pull delivery carts in cities. Today its jumping ability and great courage means it is in demand as a riding horse, while its stamina and extravagant trot make it ideal for the show ring. The Welsh Cob is very hardy and has a robust constitution, so it is quite easy to keep.

COUNTRY: Britain
BLOOD TEMPERATURE: Warm
HEIGHT: 14.2 hands and over
COLOUR: All solid colours
ENVIRONMENT: Temperate lowlands
USES: Harness, riding
TEMPERAMENT: Good natured and calm
DESCRIPTION: Neat elegant head set on an arched neck, low powerful shoulders, compact body with a deep girth, well-muscled quarters and a high-set tail

DANISH WARMBLOOD

COUNTRY: Denmark
BLOOD TEMPERATURE: Warm
HEIGHT: 16–16.2 hands
COLOUR: All solid colours
ENVIRONMENT: Cool temperate
USES: Riding, dressage
TEMPERAMENT: Amenable, intelligent
DESCRIPTION: Fine head on a muscular well-set neck, broad deep chest, sloping shoulders, compact back, well-set tail, muscular legs

Denmark has a tradition of horse breeding, both at the ancient monastic studs at Holstein – which date back to the 14th century when this area was under Danish rule – and the Frederiksborg Royal Stud. A recent purpose-bred competition horse, the Danish Warmblood has already won international recognition although the stud book was only begun in the 1960s. The base stock was local Holstein and Frederiksborg, but many other breeds were used in the programme, including Trakehner, Thoroughbred and Selle Français. The result is a versatile horse that is bold and spirited with a wonderful free action; it is ideal for jumping, dressage and other competition riding. The Dutch Warmblood has the Thoroughbred's looks but is more solid and has a better temperament. Each stallion is thoroughly tested before it is selected for inclusion in the stud book, which keeps the breed standards high.

FREDERIKSBORG

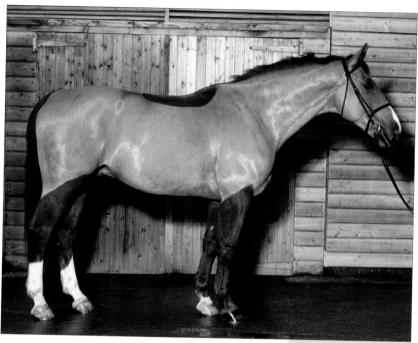

Named for King Frederik II, who founded the Frederiksborg Royal Stud in 1562, the Frederiksborg is one of Denmark's oldest breeds. Using native horses crossed with imported Spanish and Italian breeds, the Frederiksborg was intended as a versatile horse for the cavalry and as a harness horse to pull royal coaches. In the early 1700s selective breeding was introduced and one famous horse that resulted was Pluto, foaled in 1765, who became the foundation sire for one of the Lipizzaner lines. The Frederiksborg became so popular that many of the best horses were exported, so valuable breeding stock was lost nearly causing the extinction of the breed. At the end of the 1930s efforts began to re-establish the breed, although numbers are still low. The Frederiksborg has been used to improve and develop many other breeds, including the Danish Jutland and the Danish Warmblood.

COUNTRY: Denmark
BLOOD TEMPERATURE: Warm
HEIGHT: 15.3–16 hands
COLOUR: Chestnut, often with flaxen mane and tail, sometimes other colours
ENVIRONMENT: Cool temperate
USES: Riding, Harness
TEMPERAMENT: Lively and intelligent
DESCRIPTION: Well-proportioned head on a muscular upright neck, rather upright shoulders, long straight back, broad chest, rounded quarters, well-set tail

KNABSTRUP

COUNTRY: Denmark
BLOOD TEMPERATURE: Warm
HEIGHT: Averages 15.2 hands
COLOUR: Spotted
ENVIRONMENT: Cool temperate
USES: Riding, harness
TEMPERAMENT: Good natured and tractable
DESCRIPTION: Small attractive head, short thick arched neck, upright shoulder, long straight back, muscular quarters, strong short legs

The original Knabstrup breed was descended from a Spanish mare, Flaebehoppen, which was bred to Frederiksborgs on the Knabstrup estate; her grandson, Mikkel, became the foundation sire for the line of spotted horses. These early horses were robust and workmanlike, very intelligent and quick to learn, but the breed deteriorated due to poor selection – the unusual spotted coloration was considered more important than conformation. Numbers fell until the breed's survival was endangered, but in 1933 a Danish veterinarian founded an association for its preservation and numbers began to revive – although it is still quite rare. The modern Knabstrup is an animal of much better quality and a wider range of colours. It is highly intelligent, so it is often used by circus performers to carry out tricks – while its wide back makes it ideal as a base for gymnastics.

CAMARGUE

The 'horse of the sea' is indigenous to the Rhône delta of southwest France, where it roams free in what is now the Camargue National Park. The Camargue horse is perhaps descended from the prehistoric Solutré horse, and it bears a resemblance to animals in the Lascaux cave paintings dating back to 15,000 BC. Originally the horses of this region were influenced by Barbs brought by the invading Moors, but isolation means the bloodline has been untouched for centuries. The Camargue survives on reeds and rough grass and the harsh, watery environment has made it tough. It is the traditional mount of the local cowboys when they work the wild black bulls of the area, which are used for bull fights. The breed's walk is high stepping, and the canter and gallop are flowing, but the trot is so stilted that it is rarely used. Foals are born dark brown or black, but lighten to the traditional grey as they mature.

COUNTRY: France
BLOOD TEMPERATURE: Warm
HEIGHT: Up to 14.2 hands
COLOUR: Grey
ENVIRONMENT: Marshland
USES: Riding
TEMPERAMENT: Generally good-natured
DESCRIPTION: Heavy head with pronounced jaw, short neck, upright shoulders, short thickset body, short legs, high-set tail

FRENCH TROTTER

The French Trotter was once sometimes known as the Norman Trotter because of the Norman base stock in its bloodline, which was crossed with Thoroughbred, Norfolk Trotter and Standardbred. Early examples of the breed were quite heavy and resembled their Norman ancestors, but since then the French Trotter has become lighter and more refined. Bred specifically for trotting races, the French Trotter has an unusual diagonal gait when trotting, but its stamina and long stride ensure it is able to compete at the highest levels. Since it is bred for function rather than aesthetics, the conformation of the French Trotter can be quite variable but efforts have been made to achieve sloping shoulders, since they allow a longer stride. The first trotting races took place in France in the early half of the 19th century, after which the sport rapidly gained in popularity.

COUNTRY: France
BLOOD TEMPERATURE: Warm
HEIGHT: 16.2 hands
COLOUR: All solid colours, often bay or chestnut
ENVIRONMENT: Cool temperate
USES: Harness
TEMPERAMENT: Generally good natured
DESCRIPTION: Varies, but generally plain large head, proportional neck, well-set sloping shoulders, broad strong back, muscular quarters, good legs

SELLE FRANÇAIS

COUNTRY: France
BLOOD TEMPERATURE: Warm
HEIGHT: Up to 17 hands
COLOUR: All solid colours
ENVIRONMENT: Cool temperate
USES: Riding
TEMPERAMENT: Easy-going and calm
DESCRIPTION: Small attractive head on a long muscular neck, broad deep chest, relatively sloping shoulders, straight back, muscular slightly sloping quarters

During the 19th century, breeders in Normandy in northwest France imported English Thoroughbreds and Norfolk Trotters to breed with Norman horses. The local animals had considerable power and stamina and in the past had been used as war horses, but the new blood added refinement and led to two new lines: the French Trotter and the Anglo-Norman. The Anglo-Norman was further developed after the Second World War and in 1958 became the Selle Français, or French Saddle horse. The Selle Français is still a mix of breeds, with Thoroughbred, Anglo-Arab, French Trotter and Selle Français stallions used as sires. The breed has a particular talent for jumping and has won both Olympic gold and the World Showjumping Championships, but it is also excellent at dressage and eventing and is fast enough to race in categories that exclude the Thoroughbred.

BAVARIAN WARMBLOOD

Bavaria is one of the oldest horse breeding areas of Germany, but the Bavarian Warmblood is not well known although it can trace its ancestry back to the Crusades in the 11th century. It was known then as the Rottaler and was praised as an excellent warhorse. In the 18th century the Rottaler was bred with the Holstein, Andalusian and Cleveland Bay, amongst others, and in the 19th century Oldenburg blood was added to the mix, and later Thoroughbred. The aim was to achieve a lighter horse, more suitable for riding and competition than the old, heavy Rottaler. The Bavarian Warmblood has had a studbook since 1963, and breeders aim to produce a versatile horse. Temperament is important, but stock is also selected for performance – the breed is not fast, but is excellent at dressage and jumping. The Bavarian Warmblood has the lovely chestnut colour of the Rottaler.

COUNTRY: Germany
BLOOD TEMPERATURE: Warm
HEIGHT: Averages 16 hands
COLOUR: Chestnut, bay
ENVIRONMENT: Cool temperate
USES: Riding
TEMPERAMENT: Calm and good natured
DESCRIPTION: Good elegant head on a well-muscled neck, deep wide chest, long sloping shoulders, long back, powerful quarters, sturdy legs

HANOVERIAN

The Hanoverian originated in Lower Saxony in northern Germany, an area that was once the kingdom of Hanover. In 1735 George Louis, the Elector of Germany and King George II of England, founded a stud at Celle, which bred Holstein stallions with local mares to develop a horse suitable for carriage work, agricultural work and also riding. Later Thoroughbreds were added to the breeding programme to improve the quality. The first Hanoverian stud book was opened in 1888, but after the Second World War horses were less used in harness and on farms, so breeders aimed to make the Hanoverian more suitable for riding. This was done by introducing Thoroughbred blood for better conformation and more speed, as well as Trakehner to give extra strength and stamina. The modern Hanoverian is one of the best known European warmbloods and is an excellent competition horse, particularly in the fields of dressage and showjumping.

COUNTRY: Germany
BLOOD TEMPERATURE: Warm
HEIGHT: 16.2 hands
COLOUR: All solid colours
ENVIRONMENT: Cool temperate
USES: Riding
TEMPERAMENT: Calm and good natured
DESCRIPTION: Attractive head with long neck, wide deep chest, good sloping shoulders, straight back and powerful body, muscular quarters, well-set tail

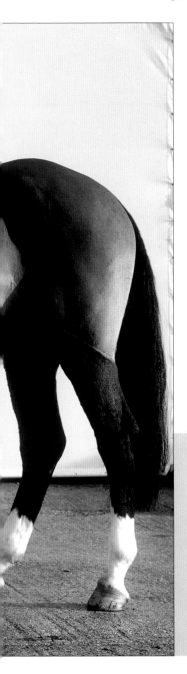

HOLSTEIN

The history of the Holstein goes back to the 13th century, when the monastery at Uetersen in the Schleswig-Holstein area was given grazing rights on nearby land by Gerhard, Count of Holstein and Storman. The monks bred horses, crossing the local stock with Spanish and oriental breeds to develop a heavy but elegant horse that was used both as a warhorse and by local farmers. The Holstein was immensely popular in the 17th and 18th centuries, then in the 19th century breeds such as the Yorkshire Coach Horse and the Cleveland Bay were introduced into the programme to create a smarter horse for carriage driving. After the Second World War the emphasis was on producing a riding horse, so Thoroughbred blood was added to the mix. Today the Holstein is one of the great sports horses and it is often used to influence other breeds.

COUNTRY: Germany
BLOOD TEMPERATURE: Warm
HEIGHT: 16–17 hands
COLOUR: All solid colours but mostly bay or chestnut
ENVIRONMENT: Cool temperate
USES: Riding
TEMPERAMENT: Easy-going, calm
DESCRIPTION: Nicely proportioned head on an elegant muscular neck, broad deep chest, sloping shoulders, straight back with muscular quarters, short legs

OLDENBURG

COUNTRY: Germany
BLOOD TEMPERATURE: Warm
HEIGHT: 16–17.2 hands
COLOUR: All solid colours, but mainly black, brown or grey
ENVIRONMENT: Cool temperate
USES: Riding, harness
TEMPERAMENT: Good natured and calm
DESCRIPTION: Quality head, sometimes with a convex profile, well-set muscular neck, powerful shoulders, broad deep chest, long back, muscular quarters

The Oldenburg was developed in the 17th century as a coach horse that was also good for agricultural work; it was based on the Friesian crossed with Spanish, Neapolitan and Turkish breeds as well as the Barb. The early Oldenburg was heavy and powerful, but had a good temperament and was very willing to work. In the 19th century it was popular with the military as a cavalry horse and with the postal service to pull heavy mail coaches. Towards the end of the 19th century requirements changed and a lighter horse was needed, so the Oldenburg was bred to the Thoroughbred to improve its quality. The modern Oldenburg is a versatile horse, although it is still one of the most powerfully-built and heaviest of the warmbloods. It is in great demand as a competition horse and is well suited for dressage, show jumping and eventing.

RHINELANDER

The Rhineland Heavy Draft was once a very popular workhorse, considered to be one of the best German coldbloods, but as the demand for horses to work the land declined breeders began to use the Rhineland Heavy Draft as a basis on which to develop a riding horse. Warmbloods that had Thoroughbred, Trakehner and Hanoverian blood were crossed with stallions from the Hanover-Westphalia area and the resulting stallions were bred back to lighter examples of the Rhineland Heavy Draft. Breeders concentrated on improving both the conformation and the action, while at the same time retaining the old Rhinelander's excellent temperament. The Rhinelander is now a useful riding horse and is particularly good at show jumping. It is becoming better known around the world, although it is not yet as famous as some of the other German breeds.

COUNTRY: Germany
BLOOD TEMPERATURE: Warm
HEIGHT: Averages 16.2 hands
COLOUR: All solid colours, but mainly chestnut
ENVIRONMENT: Cool temperate
USES: Riding
TEMPERAMENT: Easy-going, calm
DESCRIPTION: Quality head on a fairly short neck, sloping shoulders, deep broad chest, sturdy body, good legs

WESTPHALIAN

As far back as Roman times there were wild horses living in herds in Westphalia, in marshy land unsuitable for farming – even today, one of these herds still exists in the area, near Duelman, and stallions are captured and auctioned off annually. Although breeders in early times used these horses as base stock they did not establish a consistent breed standard until 1826, when the state stud was founded at Warendorf. At first Oldenburg and Anglo-Norman blood was used in the new breeding programme, but later the Westphalian was based on Hanoverian blood, with some Thoroughbred and Trakehner. In many ways the Westphalian is very similar to the Hanoverian. It is a fine competition horse, with attractive looks, and is easy to train – it excels at both show jumping and dressage. It has a fine calm temperament, which also makes it suitable for general pleasure riding.

COUNTRY: Germany
BLOOD TEMPERATURE: Warm
HEIGHT: 15.3–16.2 hands
COLOUR: All solid colours
ENVIRONMENT: Cool temperate
USES: Riding, dressage
TEMPERAMENT: Calm and good natured
DESCRIPTION: Attractive head with long neck, wide deep chest, good sloping shoulders, straight back and powerful body, muscular quarters, well-set tail

WÜRTTEMBERG

COUNTRY: Germany
BLOOD TEMPERATURE: warm
HEIGHT: 16 hands or more
COLOUR: Brown, bay, chestnut
ENVIRONMENT: Cool temperate
USES: Riding
TEMPERAMENT: Easy-going, sociable
DESCRIPTION: Medium-size horse with average head and alert ears, muscular neck, deep and broad chest, long straight back and strong legs

One of Germany's classic breeds, the Württemberg originated at the state stud of Marbach in Württemberg during the 17th century. The original version of the breed was developed by crossing local warmblood mares with Arab, Trakehner and Anglo-Norman stallions, later adding Friesian, Spanish, Barb and Suffolk Punch blood. At first the Württemberg was a small, sturdy horse built more like a cob and used for light draft and agricultural work, but later a lighter version of the breed was developed that was more suitable for riding. Unlike other German warmbloods, the Württemberg has a great deal of Arab blood since Marbach has a famous herd of Arabs. Although it is still rather a plain, stocky horse, it has an excellent action and an easy-going disposition, so it makes a great riding horse and also excels at jumping and dressage.

DUTCH WARMBLOOD

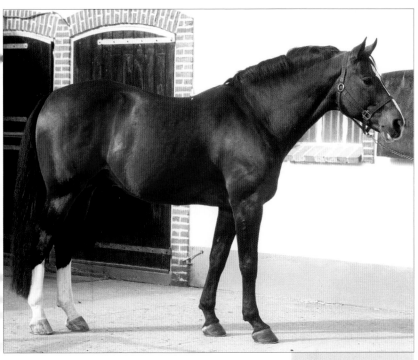

The Netherlands has a fine reputation for horse breeding and the Dutch Warmblood is one of the newest breeds developed here. It dates from after the Second World War and was intended from the first as a competition horse. Breeders began by crossing two local breeds: the Gelderland, which is an eye-catching carriage horse and gave size, strength and a showy action, and the Groningen, a heavier horse with lots of power, stamina and endurance. Later some Thoroughbred blood was included to give refinement and speed, although only in small amounts because of its excitable temperament. The Dutch Warmblood is noted for its sound limbs and although it is not the fastest horse it is athletic with an excellent jumping ability. It is very attractive and has a wonderful free-flowing action and an amenable temperament, which also makes it ideal for dressage.

COUNTRY: Netherlands
BLOOD TEMPERATURE: Warm
HEIGHT: Up to 16.3 hands
COLOUR: All solid colours
ENVIRONMENT: Cool temperate
USES: Riding, dressage
TEMPERAMENT: Good natured and amenable
DESCRIPTION: Well-proportioned head, muscular well-set neck, deep broad chest, sloping shoulders, straight back, powerful quarters and well-set tail

FRIESIAN

The now extinct Forest Horse was a massive animal and it is believed that monks in the Friesland area of the Netherlands may have bred it to lighter types to create the ancestor of the Friesian. It is certain that this elegant, glossy black horse carried knights to the crusades – the breed is very strong for its size and has a proud bearing. In the 16–17th centuries, when the Spanish occupied the Netherlands, the Friesian was probably bred to Spanish horses – the influence of the Andalusian and the Lusitano has led to the luxuriant mane and tail and the high-stepping action. The Romans took the Friesian to Britain, where it influenced the Dales and Fell ponies and was used to develop the now extinct English Great Horse – which was an ancestor of the Shire Horse. The Friesian is noted for its amenable temperament and willing nature and excels as a carriage horse.

COUNTRY: Netherlands
BLOOD TEMPERATURE: Cold
HEIGHT: 15–16.3 hands
COLOUR: Black
ENVIRONMENT: Cool temperate
USES: Harness
TEMPERAMENT: Docile and good natured
DESCRIPTION: Aristocratic head on a powerful arched neck, strong shoulders, compact body, short strong legs with thick silky feathering, luxuriant mane and tail

GELDERLAND

COUNTRY: Netherlands
BLOOD TEMPERATURE: Warm
HEIGHT: 15.2–16.2 hands
COLOUR: Mainly chestnut
ENVIRONMENT: Cool temperate
USES: Riding, harness, light draft
TEMPERAMENT: Easy-going
DESCRIPTION: Long rather plain head, muscular gently curving neck, rather straight shoulders, straight back with muscular quarters, high-set tail

Gelderland is a region of the Netherlands and in the 19th century breeders began to developed a horse for local farmers both versatile enough to be ridden and used as a carriage horse. The Gelderland was based on local mares, bred to Norfolk Trotter, Andalusian and Holstein stallions, among others – initially the gene pool was quite varied. Later, East Friesian, Oldenburg, Hackney and Thoroughbred blood was also added. After the mechanization of agriculture the Gelderland was used less on the farm, but was valued as a showy carriage horse with an excellent temperament. It was used to develop the Dutch Warmblood, with the Groningen, and since the 1960s it has been classed as a category of the Dutch Warmblood. It is still used as an elegant carriage horse, and its high-stepping trot is good for competitive driving – where it competes at high levels although it is not particularly fast.

GRONINGEN

Currently quite rare, the Groningen was once widely found in the Netherlands where it was valued as a reliable workhorse that was sturdy enough to keep going all day. Although it did not have the looks of the neighbouring Gelderland it was a much heavier animal, which made it more suitable to work the clay soils of the Groningen province. It was developed by crossing the local stock with Friesian and Oldenburg, and later Suffolk Punch was added to the mix for more weight and additional strength. Along with the Gelderland it was used to develop the Dutch Warmblood, which was so successful that by 1970 only one purebred Groningen stallion remained. Oldenburg blood was again used to save the breed and although, like the Gelderland, it is currently classed as a category of the Dutch Warmblood, the Groningen still survives.

COUNTRY: Netherlands
BLOOD TEMPERATURE: Warm
HEIGHT: 15.3–16.1 hands
COLOUR: Bay, brown, black
ENVIRONMENT: Cool temperate
USES: Agriculture, harness, light draft
TEMPERAMENT: Calm and willing
DESCRIPTION: Long plain head, muscular neck, slightly sloping shoulders, broad deep chest, long back, muscular quarters, high-set tail, short strong legs

SWEDISH WARMBLOOD

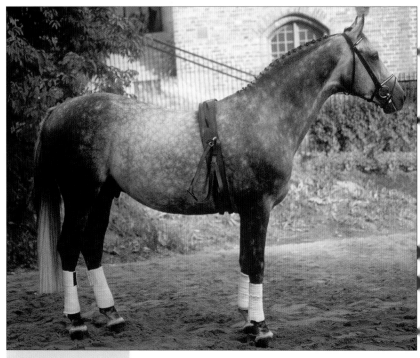

COUNTRY: Sweden
BLOOD TEMPERATURE: Warm
HEIGHT: Around 16.3 hands
COLOUR: All solid colours
ENVIRONMENT: Temperate
USES: Riding, dressage, harness
TEMPERAMENT: Well balanced and calm
DESCRIPTION: Attractive head on a long well-formed neck, muscular and sloping shoulders, broad deep chest, compact body, muscular quarters

Originating in the 17th century, the Swedish Warmblood was intended as a cavalry horse. The great Swedish studs of Strömsholm and Flyinge, both founded in the 1600s, bred local mares to a wide range of other breeds and created horses for local farmers and for the military. When the military initiated their own breeding programme they imported Friesians, Thoroughbreds, Hanoverians and Trakehners, and created a versatile, quality riding horse. In 1874, the government introduced selective breeding and established standards for several new breeds, including the Swedish Warmblood. The Swedish Warmblood Association was formed in 1928 and rigorous approvals improved the breed further. The Swedish Warmblood is valued for its looks, sensible temperament and excellent abilities. It excels at jumping, dressage, eventing and driving.

SWISS WARMBLOOD OR EINSIEDLER

The Swiss Warmblood is also called the Einsiedler, since it originates from the Benedictine Monastery of Einsiedeln – the monasteries of Europe played a large part in the development of many European breeds. In the 10th century the monks of Einsiedeln were breeding a versatile horse to work the land and to ride, and by the Middle Ages they had developed a superior horse known as the Cavalli della Madonna. It was later renamed the Einsiedler and by 1655 a studbook was opened. Later in the 17th century crosses were tried with a variety of other breeds, but this had a detrimental effect. By 1784 a new studbook had been initiated, and despite a continuing diversity of influences the Swiss Warmblood developed its own distinct characteristics. Versatile and attractive, it is suitable for most kinds of competitive riding, as well as driving in harness.

COUNTRY: Switzerland
BLOOD TEMPERATURE: Warm
HEIGHT: Up to 16.2 hands
COLOUR: Mainly chestnut or bay, can be any solid colour
ENVIRONMENT: Temperate mountain
USES: Riding, harness
TEMPERAMENT: Generally good-natured
DESCRIPTION: Well-proportioned head, muscular neck, broad deep chest, sloping shoulders, long straight back, powerful quarters, long legs

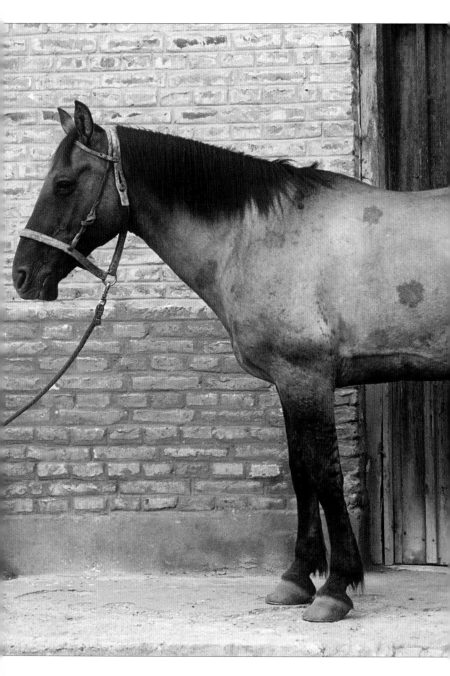

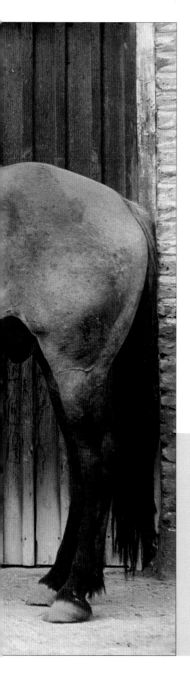

CRIOLLO

The native horse of Argentina, the Criollo dates back to the 16th century when Spanish horses – with mainly Barb blood – were imported into Buenos Aires. They were bred to native stock, but in the mid-16th century the Indians sacked the city and many horses escaped to run wild. The local climate is harsh, with extremes of temperature, and the Criollo developed into a hardy animal, with great endurance and stamina. By the beginning of the 19th century the breed was in danger from contamination by outside blood, which was having a detrimental effect, so a society was established to preserve it. The Criollo is valued for its amazing longevity and stamina and is a particularly frugal eater. It is the favoured mount of the gaucho, the local cowboy, and played an important part in the development of the Argentinian polo pony.

COUNTRY: Argentina
BLOOD TEMPERATURE: Warm
HEIGHT: 14–15 hands
COLOUR: Mostly dun, but can be any colour
ENVIRONMENT: Grasslands
USES: Riding
TEMPERAMENT: Willing, easy-going
DESCRIPTION: Long head on a long muscular neck, sloping shoulder, broad chest, compact back with muscular quarters, strong legs

MANGALARGA MARCHADOR

COUNTRY: Brazil
BLOOD TEMPERATURE: Warm
HEIGHT: 14.2–16 hands
COLOUR: Mostly grey, bay and chestnut
ENVIRONMENT: Grassland
USES: Riding, ranching, harness
TEMPERAMENT: Docile and calm
DESCRIPTION: Attractive head on an elegant curving neck, deep chest, well-proportioned body, muscular quarters, low-set tail, powerful legs

Originally called the Sublime, the Mangalarga Marchador originated in the mid-18th century in Brazil. A Spanish stallion, Sublime – who was possibly an Alter-Real – was presented to the Baron of Aldenas in 1812. The stallion was bred to mares with the blood of the now extinct Spanish Jennet and the Barb, and the progeny were first called after their sire. Later the Hacienda Mangalarga acquired some of the stock and continued the breeding programme. The Mangalarga Marchador has many characteristics inherited from the Jennet, including a particularly smooth action. It has three gaits: the *marcha picada*, a smooth lateral pace with little vertical movement that is particularly comfortable; the *marcha batida*, a diagonal four-beat gait similar to the foxtrot, and the centre march, a smooth canter. The breed is very versatile with a calm temperament, so it is suitable for children and novices.

PERUVIAN PASO

The Peruvian Paso is also known as the Peruvian Stepping Horse and is descended from horses taken to Peru in the first half of the 16th century. These were almost certainly Barb and Andalusian, but also Spanish Jennet since the Peruvian Paso is another naturally gaited horse. Very few other breeds were involved in its development, and the Paso not only has the smoothest gait but can be guaranteed to pass it on to its progeny. The unique lateral gait of the breed is supremely smooth for the rider and covers a great deal of ground. It also has a unique pace called the *termino*, in which the foreleg moves out to the side and down, rather like a swimming movement. Although the gait of the Peruvian Paso is very important, breeders in Peru have also selected for temperament so it is a willing horse – although it certainly does not lack spirit.

COUNTRY: Peru
BLOOD TEMPERATURE: Warm
HEIGHT: 14–15 hands
COLOUR: All solid colours
ENVIRONMENT: Savannah
USES: Riding
TEMPERAMENT: Willing but lively
DESCRIPTION: Quality head on an arched muscular neck, compact body, deep girth, muscular quarters, strong legs and feet

PASO FINO

The Paso Fino is descended from the Spanish horses brought to South America by the conquistadors in the 16th century and it developed in the Dominican Republic, Puerto Rico, Venezuela, Cuba and Columbia. It is believed to be a mix of the now extinct Spanish Jennet, the Andalusian and perhaps the Barb. 'Paso fino' literally means 'fine walk' and the four-beat gait of this breed is natural – new born foals can exhibit it shortly after birth. There are three different speeds of gait: the *paso fino* is the slowest in terms of forward motion, although the feet move up and down very fast; the *paso corto* is a ground-covering gait, very smooth and a similar speed to a trot; the *paso largo* is a fast gait somewhere between a canter and a gallop – speeds of up to 22 mph (35.2 km/h) can be achieved.

COUNTRY: Peru
BLOOD TEMPERATURE: Warm
HEIGHT: 14–15 hands
COLOUR: All solid colours
ENVIRONMENT: Grasslands
USES: Riding
TEMPERAMENT: Amenable but lively
DESCRIPTION: Neat well-shaped head on a muscular neck, powerful shoulders, broad deep chest, short back, rounded quarters, strong legs

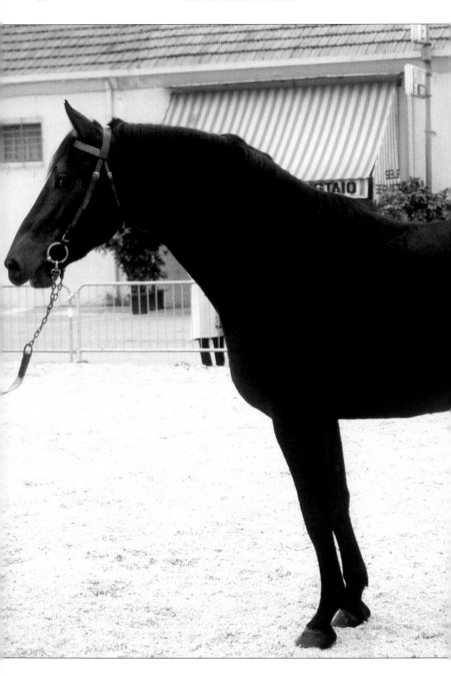

CALABRESE

Horses were bred in Italy before the founding of Rome, but the Calabrese dates back to the beginning of the 18th century. It originated in Calabria, right down in the southernmost toe of Italy, as a result of crossing Arabs with Andalusian horses. The new breed was popular with knights as it was strong, but spirited, but local farmers preferred the mule, which was thought to work harder and cope with the terrain better. Although Calabrese decreased in numbers it did not disappear, and was revived again in the 19th century, when the addition of Thoroughbred blood added refinement. Today the Calabrese is a useful all-round riding horse with a good temperament; it is a tough and hardy breed and although quite manageable can be active and energetic when required. It is not widely known worldwide, but is reasonably popular in its native land.

COUNTRY: Italy
BLOOD TEMPERATURE: Warm
HEIGHT: 15.3–16.2 hands
COLOUR: All solid colours
ENVIRONMENT: Mediterranean
USES: Riding
TEMPERAMENT: Calm, active
DESCRIPTION: Refined head, well-proportioned neck, broad deep chest, sloping shoulders, compact body with short muscular back, muscular quarters

MAREMMANA

COUNTRY: Italy
BLOOD TEMPERATURE: Warm
HEIGHT: 15–15.3 hands
COLOUR: All solid colours
ENVIRONMENT: Mediterranean
USES: Riding, light draft
TEMPERAMENT: Generally good-natured
DESCRIPTION: Long heavy plain head, short muscular neck, slightly sloping shoulders, short straight back, strong legs and hard feet

A native of Tuscany, the Maremmana takes its name from Maremma , a region of marshland on the coast. The origins of the breed are not clear, since there has been much crossbreeding over the years. It is clear there is some Barb blood in the mix, giving hardiness, great stamina and a tenacious spirtit, and also Norfolk Trotter, which improved the action. The Maremma is a general-purpose riding horse, but is also a favoured mount of the police and once of the cavalry. However, the breed excels at working cattle and is used by Italy's version of the cowboy, the *butteri*, to herd the local buffalo and cattle of the region. The Maremmana has had little planned breeding and is not a handsome horse, but it is versatile, calm and a good worker. Recently it has been finding a new career in the tourist industry, trekking across the countryside.

MURGESE

The exact history of the Murgese is not certain, but it first developed around the 15th century; during this century and the following it was popular as a cavalry horse. It is likely that the bloodline contained elements of Neapolitan, Barb and Arab, and maybe some Avelignese, and the breed took its name from the area of Murge in the region of Puglia in Italy. Later it fell into decline and almost became extinct, but in the 1920s renewed interest led to the breed becoming re-established – although it is not certain that the modern Murgese bears much relation to its ancestor. It is almost certainly more refined after the addition of Thoroughbred blood. The Murgese is tough but very good-natured and economical to keep. It is still used in agriculture and for light draft, but is also gaining popularity as a riding horse.

COUNTRY: Italy
BLOOD TEMPERATURE: Warm
HEIGHT: 15–16 hands
COLOUR: Mostly chestnut or black, occasionally grey
ENVIRONMENT: Mediterranean
USES: Light draft, riding
TEMPERAMENT: Calm, good-natured
DESCRIPTION: Attractive convex head, muscular neck with a full mane, deep broad chest, slightly sloping shoulder, short back, strong legs

SALERNO

COUNTRY: Italy
BLOOD TEMPERATURE: Warm
HEIGHT: 16–17 hands
COLOUR: All solid colours
ENVIRONMENT: Mediterranan
USES: Riding
TEMPERAMENT: Good-natured and easy-going
DESCRIPTION: Well-set quality head, long muscular neck, well-proportioned back, sloping shoulder, muscular quarters, slender legs

Unfortunately the Salerno is quite rare, although it has some excellent qualities. It is an old breed, dating back to the latter half of the 18th century when it was first developed at the Persano stud in the Campania region of Italy. Here Neapolitans were crossed with local horses, with some added Arab and Spanish blood, and the breed initially took the name of the stud. After the stud closed in 1864, the breed became known as the Salerno. The Salerno has a calm temperament, good conformation, and makes an excellent riding horse, but it also has a very athletic jump and excels at show jumping. Two of the greatest Italian show jumpers were Salernos: Merano, who won the World Show Jumping Championships in 1956, and Posillipo, who rode to gold at the 1960 Olympics – both ridden by Raimondo d'Inzeo.

SAN FRATELLO

The San Fratello is the closest thing Italy has to a wild horse; a herd roams semi-wild on the wooded slopes of the Nebrodi Mountains in the province of Messina in eastern Sicily. Its exact bloodline is unknown – it probably has elements of Thoroughbred and oriental blood, mixed with that of local breeds such as the Murgese and the Salerno. The harsh nature of its environment, which ranges from cold in winter to hot and humid in summer, has given the breed an excellent constitution and it is resistant to many equine diseases. In the Middle Ages it carried knights into battle and was used by local farmers to work the land. There are now only a few hundred San Fratello left, but since the 1990s a herdbook has been kept and the Italian government has pledged an interest in preserving this unique breed.

COUNTRY: Italy
BLOOD TEMPERATURE: Warm
HEIGHT: 15–16 hands
COLOUR: Bay, black
ENVIRONMENT: Mediterranean
USES: Riding
TEMPERAMENT: Easy-going and calm
DESCRIPTION: Attractive but slightly heavy head, muscular but rather short neck, broad deep chest, gently sloping shoulders, muscular quarters with high-set tail

ALTER-REAL

Although it was developed as a horse fit for royalty, the Alter-Real has had a varied history. It was founded in the mid-18th century when the royal Braganza family imported Andalusion mares to establish a royal stud, to provide horses for displays of advanced classical horsemanship, or *haute école*, and for carriage work. The Alter-Real breed soon became famous, but in the early 19th century much of the best stock was lost when Napoleon invaded. Later the pure bloodline was contaminated with foreign blood, with disastrous effects. Andalusians were again used to revive the breed, but then the stud archives were destroyed when the Portuguese monarchy was dissolved in 1910. Luckily equine expert Dr Ruy D'Andrade saved two stallions and due to his efforts the breed survived; since 1932 the breeding programme has been run by the Portuguese Ministry of Agriculture. The Alter-Real is an intelligent horse with a distinctive character and a showy action, ideal for the *haute école*.

COUNTRY: Portugal
BLOOD TEMPERATURE: Warm
HEIGHT: 15–16 hands
COLOUR: Bay, brown grey, sometimes chestnut
ENVIRONMENT: Southern temperate
USES: Riding
TEMPERAMENT: Intelligent, can be temperamental
DESCRIPTION: Average size head with either a straight or convex profile, short muscular arched neck, compact body, muscular quarters with well-set tail

LIPIZZANER

Although the Lipizzaner originates from Slovenia, it is firmly associated with the Spanish Riding School in Vienna – 'Spanish' because it features Spanish horses. The Lipizzaner was first developed at a stud at Lipica (formerly Lipizza) in Slovenia, which was founded in 1580 by Archduke Charles II, son of the Austrian emperor Ferdinand I. Here Andalusians and Barbs were crossed with local horses – which although small, were tough with a high-stepping gait. The Lipizzaner is almost invariably grey, but foals are born dark brown or black and their coat lightens as they grow older. However, some do remain dark and traditionally there is always one bay at the Spanish Riding School. The best horses are trained to appear at the school, performing amazing feats of horsemanship – the renowned 'airs above the ground'. However the Lipizzaner is also popular as a dressage horse, and some animals are used on the farm and for general riding.

COUNTRY: Slovenia
BLOOD TEMPERATURE: Warm
HEIGHT: 15–16 hands
COLOUR: Almost always grey
ENVIRONMENT: Cool temperate
USES: Riding, harness
TEMPERAMENT: Intelligent, willing, good-natured
DESCRIPTION: Large attractive head on a short crested neck, deep chest, sloping shoulders, compact body, powerful rounded quarters, well-set tail

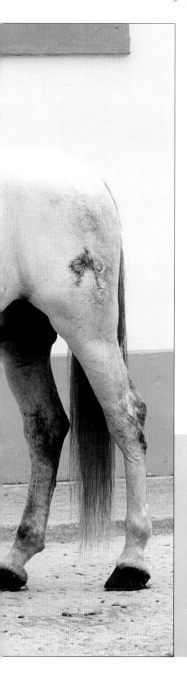

ANDALUSIAN

Cave paintings in southern Spain dating back to 20,000 BC show the prehistoric ancestor of the Andalusian. The breed as we know it today was based on these horses, and it has since spread around the world and had a major influence on many other breeds, including the Lipizzaner, Hackney, Criollo and the Quarter Horse. Once the Andalusian was the mount of kings, but it briefly fell out of favour in the Middle Ages, when heavier horses were required to carry knights in their heavy armour. In the 15th century firearms were invented and the Andalusian became popular again, particularly as its proud beauty was ideal for the *haute école*. One of Spain's most famous horses, the Andalusian has amazing presence, an extravagant high-stepping gait, and is agile and athletic. It is still known as the Andalusian around the world, but in Spain itself the breed is now called Pura Raza Española – the pure Spanish breed.

COUNTRY: Spain
BLOOD TEMPERATURE: Warm
HEIGHT: 15–16 hands
COLOUR: Mostly grey, can be bay, black, chestnut or roan
ENVIRONMENT: Southern temperate
USES: Riding
TEMPERAMENT: Usually good-natured, can be temperamental
DESCRIPTION: Attractive head with broad forehead and convex nose, thick arched neck, sloping shoulders, broad deep chest, muscular quarters, long thick mane and tail

CARTHUSIAN

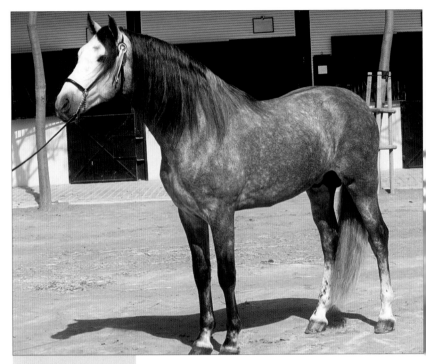

COUNTRY: Spain
BLOOD TEMPERATURE:
  Warm
HEIGHT: 15–16 hands
COLOUR: Mostly grey, can
  be bay, black, chestnut
  or roan
ENVIRONMENT: Southern
  temperate
USES: Riding
TEMPERAMENT: Usually
  good-natured, can be
  temperamental
DESCRIPTION: Fine head set
  well on an arched
  muscular neck, sloping
  shoulders, deep chest,
  well-proportioned back,
  muscular quarters

A 15th century Carthusian monastery in Andalusia is famous as the birthplace of the Carthusian horse, or Cartujano, which is the purest strain of Spanish horse. It was developed by the monks through careful selective breeding some 500 years ago and the descendants of those first Cartujanos make up the oldest dynasty of purebred horses in Europe. When the breed was in danger of extinction, the horses bred by the monastery kept it going. Today the Carthusian is classed as a branch of the Andalusian, rather than a separate breed in its own right, but it retains its own identity and it is still bred at the Fuente del Suero ranch in Jerez, within sight of the founding monastery. Foals of the Carthusian are born dark, but the coat gradually changes to grey as it matures. The breed is prized for its stamina and versatility and also for its excellent temperament.

HISPANO

The Hispano originated in Spain, as a result of crossing the Spanish Andalusian with the English Thoroughbred and the Arab – it is also known as the Spanish Anglo-Arab, which reflects this mix. Although the breed is reasonably established, it can still vary quite a lot in general appearance – depending on which ancestor is the more dominant. The Hispano is well-proportioned and is generally level-headed, courageous, fast and agile with considerable presence, so in Spain it is often used in the bullring and to train the young bulls beforehand. In other areas it is also valued as a general riding horse – the sloping shoulder gives a free-flowing action – and has been reasonable successful at both dressage and show jumping. It is not yet well known around the rest of the world and still remains fairly rare.

COUNTRY: Spain
BLOOD TEMPERATURE: Hot
HEIGHT: Up to 16 hands
COLOUR: Bay, grey, chestnut
ENVIRONMENT: Southern temperate
USES: Riding
TEMPERAMENT: Generally good, can be temperamental
DESCRIPTION: Fine head usually with a straight profile, elegant gently-curved neck, wide deep chest, sloping shoulder, straight back, muscular quarters, well-set tail

LUSITANO

In many ways the Lusitano is the Portuguese equivalent of the Spanish Andalusian, and there are only slight differences between the two breeds. Both developed from the same background, with Sorraia and Barb blood, but whereas the Andalusian also has some Arab blood – as shown by its oriental-looking head – the Lusitano is more purebred. It was originally developed as a cavalry and carriage horse, but its remarkable agility now makes it a good show ring horse – and it is highly valued as a mount for local bullfighters, for which it is schooled in the disciplines of the *haute école*. In Portuguese bullfighting the bulls are not killed, so the horse needs to be particularly fast and calm and handled with expert skill to avoid injury. The Lusitano is also used for pleasure riding and for light work around the farm. Its name comes from the Latin name for Portugal, Lusitania.

COUNTRY: Portugal
BLOOD TEMPERATURE: Warm
HEIGHT: 15–16 hands
COLOUR: All solid colours
ENVIRONMENT: Southern temperate
USES: Riding, harness
TEMPERAMENT: Intelligent, sensible, easy-going
DESCRIPTION: Attractive head, short arched neck, powerful upright shoulders, broad chest, compact back, muscular quarters, long legs

HEAVY HORSES

KLADRUBER

COUNTRY: Former
  Czechoslovakia
BLOOD TEMPERATURE:
  Cold
HEIGHT: 16.2–17 hands
COLOUR: Grey, black
ENVIRONMENT: Temperate
USES: Harness
TEMPERAMENT: Calm,
  amiable
DESCRIPTION: Long head
  with convex profile,
  muscular arched neck,
  sloping shoulders,
  deep chest, long back,
  muscular quarters,
  prolific mane and tail

During the 15–17th centuries the Kladruby Imperial
Court Stud bred a new horse that was primarily intended
as the ideal carriage horse. It was apparently based on a
mix of Neapolitan and Andalusian blood, although a fire
in 1757 destroyed most of the breeding records. The new
breed was named the Kladruber after the stud, and
originally came in a variety of coat colours – even
palomino and appaloosa – although later the breed was
restricted to grey and black. Unfortunately the black herd
was nearly destroyed in the 1930s, when many of the
horses were sold off for meat. A few were saved and the
black line was re-established in 1945 at the Slatinany stud
near the Iron Hills, using Kladruber mares and Lipizzaner
and Friesian stallions. The Kladruber is strong, with a
calm temperament, and is an excellent competitive
driving horse.

MURÄKOZI

The Muräkozi was developed in the 19–20th centuries in the area around the river Mura in southern Hungary. The breed is descended from crossing native Hungarian mares with Percheron, Ardennais and Noriker stallions – with some Arab blood added in the later stages, which gives it a quality look. The Muräkozi was noted for being strong and fast, as well as reliable and economic to keep. These qualities made it suitable for the army and it was popular as a mount for the cavalry before the First World War, as well being used as for agricultural work. Between the wars there was an increase in farming in Hungary and neighbouring Poland so the Muräkozi was bred in some numbers. Many were lost in the Second World War, and afterwards the onset of mechanization made their role almost obsolete. However, the Muräkozi is often still used for agricultural work in central and eastern Europe.

COUNTRY: Hungary
BLOOD TEMPERATURE: Cold
HEIGHT: 16 hands
COLOUR: Liver chestnut with flaxen mane and tail, bay, brown, black, grey
ENVIRONMENT: Temperate
USES: Draught
TEMPERAMENT: Generally willing and biddable
DESCRIPTION: Plain head on a short muscular neck, powerful shoulders, compact body, short strong legs with limited feathering

VLADIMIR HEAVY DRAUGHT

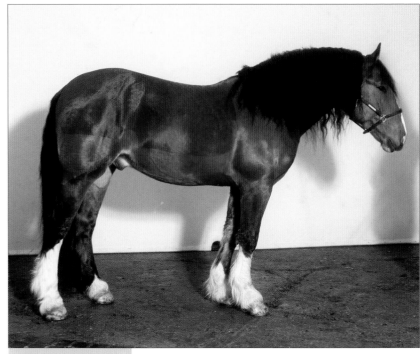

COUNTRY: Russia
BLOOD TEMPERATURE: Cold
HEIGHT: Up to 16.1 hands
COLOUR: Any solid colour, but mostly bay
ENVIRONMENT: Cool temperate
USES: Draught, harness
TEMPERAMENT: Gentle, willing
DESCRIPTION: Large head with convex or straight profile, well-proportioned muscular neck, powerful shoulders, long back, short legs with much feathering

Originally developed in the Vladimir and Ivanovo regions of Russia in the late 1800s, the Vladimir Heavy Draught was only recognized as an official breed in 1946. It was developed from crossing local mares with Clydesdale and Shire stallions, while Cleveland Bay, Percheron and Suffolk Punch blood was added later. No new blood was introduced after 1925, but by the end of the 20th century numbers had decreased to such an extent that the breed was in danger of extinction so Clydesdale and Shire stallions are once again being used to build up stocks. The Vladimir Heavy Draught is a striking horse and is known for being able to travel fast while pulling heavy loads. It is also renowned for its nimble gait and free-flowing action and is elegant when used as a harness horse – to pull the traditional Russian troika, for instance.

NORIKER

The Noriker takes its name from the ancient Roman province of Noricum, in what is now Austria, and may have been developed from a heavy warhorse that was bred in the Salzburg region. The breed dates back to 600 BC, but was not recognized until the 16th century, when it was being bred in studs attached to the monasteries and appeared in the Salzburg Stud Book first begun by the Prince-Archbishop. At this point the horses were often used for ceremonials, but were also still heavily employed by alpine farmers. The harsh conditions of the area created a horse that was tough, able to survive very bad weather, surefooted and a versatile worker. Today the breed is still valued as a powerful workhorse with an excellent temperament and a willing attitude, and very strict controls keep the breed standards high.

COUNTRY: Austria
BLOOD TEMPERATURE: Cold
HEIGHT: 15.2–17 hands
COLOUR: Liver chestnut with flaxen mane and tail, all solid colours, spotted
ENVIRONMENT: Temperate mountains
USES: Light draught
TEMPERAMENT: Easy-going, amiable
DESCRIPTION: Handsome head that can be a little heavy, strong shoulders, deep chest, rounded body, strong legs with feathering

BRABANT

Also known as the Belgian Heavy Draught, the Brabant is an ancient breed that is thought to be a direct descendant of the now extinct Forest Horse. The Brabant has a particularly pure bloodline, as Belgian breeders did not introduce foreign breeds in an attempt to develop a horse suitable for cavalry, as others had done. There were originally three principal lines – Colosses de la Mehaique, founded by the stallion Jean I, Gris de Hainaut, founded by the stallion Bayard, and Gros de la Dendre, founded by Orange I – but by the beginning of the 20th century the distinction between them had vanished. The Brabant is one of the heaviest draught horses, incredibly strong but also willing and amiable. They were extremely popular as workhorses until the advent of mechanization caused an inevitable drop in demand, but they have since become a popular breed in the United States.

COUNTRY: Belgium
BLOOD TEMPERATURE: Cold
HEIGHT: 16.2–17 hands
COLOUR: Usually roan, can be chestnut or bay
ENVIRONMENT: Temperate farmland
USES: Heavy draught
TEMPERAMENT: Easy-going, amiable
DESCRIPTION: Small head on a muscular neck, huge powerful shoulders, thick compact body, muscular quarters, short legs with some feathering at the fetlock

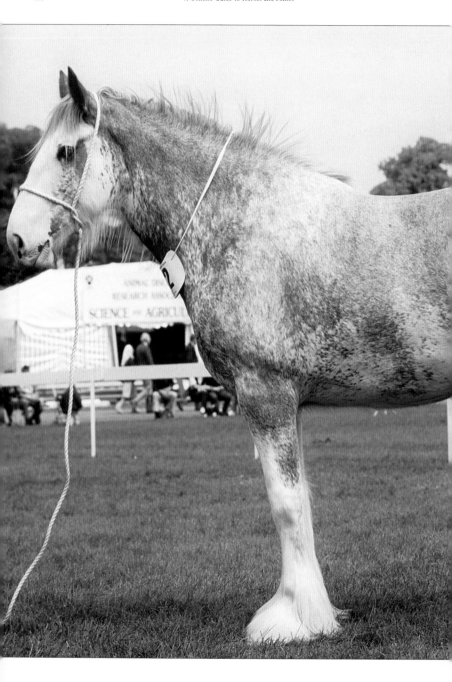

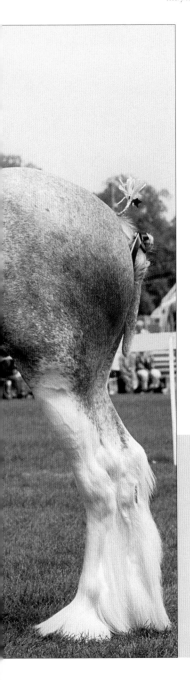

CLYDESDALE

The Clydesdale was the first draught horse to have its own society, formed in 1877. The breed originated in Scotland in the Clyde region in the early 18th century, after the 6th Duke of Hamilton imported Flemish stallions to mate with local mares to increase the size and bulk of the local draught horse. Shire horses were also used in the breeding programme – to the extent that some believed that the Shire and the Clydesdale were two lines of one breed, rather than two separate breeds. The Clydesdale was used extensively in agriculture in the region as well as for hauling loads in the coal industry, but numbers declined as mechanized transport became more usual. However, the Clydesdale is now very popular as a show horse and is often kept for pleasure, also prompting a revival in traditional skills such as harness making and shoeing.

COUNTRY: Britain
BLOOD TEMPERATURE: Cold
HEIGHT: 16–18 hands
ENVIRONMENT: Temperate farmland
USES: Draught, harness
TEMPERAMENT: Easy-going, sociable
DESCRIPTION: Attractive head with a broad forehead and straight profile, curved neck, slightly sloping shoulders, compact body, muscular quarters, strong legs with much feathering

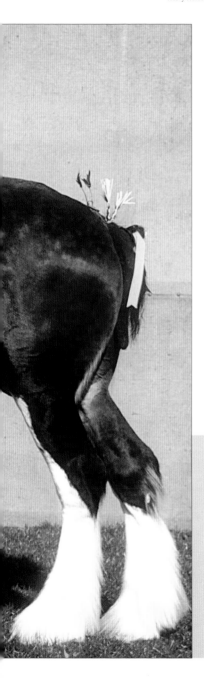

SHIRE

The name of the Shire horse comes from the British midland shires of Lincoln, Leicester, Stafford and Derby; it was said to have been named by King Henry VIII. It was another king, William the Conqueror, who brought the medieval Great Horse to England after the Norman Conquest; it was then bred to Flemish, Belgian and Friesian stallions. At first the only coat colour was black, and Oliver Cromwell dubbed the breed the English Black. Later other colours began to appear and the Shire became the breed's accepted name. Although it is a massive animal, the Shire horse is very gentle and is therefore easy to handle. It has great strength and amazing pulling power and was once widely used in agriculture. Today the breed is still massively popular – partly due to the support of breweries, which sometimes use Shires to pull their drays for urban deliveries and also take part in demonstrations and shows.

COUNTRY: Britain
BLOOD TEMPERATURE: Cold
HEIGHT: Over 17 hands
COLOUR: Chestnut, bay, grey or brown with white markings
ENVIRONMENT: Temperate farmland
USES: Heavy draught
TEMPERAMENT: Docile and gentle
DESCRIPTION: Attractive head, often with convex profile, long slightly arched neck, powerful sloping shoulders, rounded muscular quarters, long legs with heavy feathering

SUFFOLK PUNCH

COUNTRY: Britain
BLOOD TEMPERATURE: Cold
HEIGHT: Average 16.1 hands, but can be over 17 hands
COLOUR: Chestnut
ENVIRONMENT: Cool temperate
USES: Heavy draught
TEMPERAMENT: Easy-going, willing
DESCRIPTION: Large head with wide forehead, thick powerful neck, sloping muscular shoulders, deep chest, powerful quarters, quite short legs with minimal feathering

Although the colour of the Suffolk Punch is chestnut, the Suffolk Horse Society traditionally spells it 'chesnut' and recognizes seven shades: bright, red, golden, yellow, light, dark and dull dark. The Suffolk has the purest bloodline of any British heavy breed – all registered animals can trace their ancestry back through the male line to one foundation sire: Crisp's Horse of Ufford, foaled in 1768. The Suffolk Punch is quite short and unlike the other two British breeds – the Clydesdale and Shire – has little leg feathering. The soil of East Anglia in the east of Britain, where the breed developed, is heavy clay so the lack of feathering was clearly an advantage. Although a powerful and hardworking breed, the Suffolk Punch was little known outside its locality and numbers fell drastically after the Second World War. However, numbers are currently increasing, but it is still far from safe.

JUTLAND

The Jutland, Denmark's breed of heavy horse, has been bred there since the 12th century – and may go back even further to the age of the Vikings. Some believe that the Jutland was taken to England by the Vikings, and was an ancestor of the Suffolk Punch. This breed certainly had an influence on the modern Jutland, after a Suffolk Punch stallion, Oppenheim LXII, was imported in 1860 and used in the breeding programme, which was also thought to include the Cleveland Bay and the Yorkshire Coach Horse. In its turn, the Jutland was a major influence in the development of the German Schleswig Heavy Draught. Once the Jutland was a warhorse, strong and heavy enough to carry a knight in full armour, but was also used by local farmers. Now such horses are rarely ridden and are most often used by breweries for pulling drays and at shows and festivals.

COUNTRY: Denmark
BLOOD TEMPERATURE: Cold
HEIGHT: 15–16 hands
COLOUR: Chestnut, sometimes with flaxen mane and tail, can be bay, black
ENVIRONMENT: Temperate farmland
USES: Draught
TEMPERAMENT: Generally calm, willing
DESCRIPTION: Plain heavy head, high muscular neck, upright muscular shoulders, compact body with short back, short stocky legs with heavy feathering

ARDENNAIS

One of the most ancient draught breeds, the Ardennais originally came from the mountainous Ardennes area of northern France extending over into Belgium. Julius Caesar mentions the breed in accounts of his conquest of Gaul – he praised it as 'rustic, hard and tireless' and recommended it for military use; later Napoleon Bonaparte used it to transport heavy artillery and supplies and it had a similar role in both the First and Second World Wars. As well as being used as a warhorse, the Ardennais was bred for working on the land – the mountainous environment of its homeland made it naturally hardy and economical to keep. Today there are stud books for the breed in France, Belgium, Luxembourg, Sweden and Britain, all of which accept each other's horses. The Ardennais is still used for agricultural work in most areas, but in some countries it is also bred for meat.

COUNTRY: France
BLOOD TEMPERATURE: Cold
HEIGHT: Up to 16.2 hands
COLOUR: Usually roan, can be bay, chestnut, grey, palomino but not black
ENVIRONMENT: Temperate mountains
USES: Heavy draught, meat
TEMPERAMENT: Gentle and willing
DESCRIPTION: Large well-shaped head on a thickset neck, sloping shoulder, compact body, short back, short stocky legs with heavy coarse feathering

AUXOIS

COUNTRY: France
BLOOD TEMPERATURE: Cold
HEIGHT: Usually 16.3 hands and over
COLOUR: Bay, roan, chestnut
ENVIRONMENT: Temperate farmland
USES: Harness, light draught, milk, meat
TEMPERAMENT: Easy-going, gentle
DESCRIPTION: Rather small head with broad forehead, thickset neck, sloping shoulders, wide deep chest, short broad back, slender powerful legs

The Auxois is quite closely related to the Ardennais but is slightly larger and has much less feathering on the legs. A powerful horse with great endurance and pulling capacity, the breed is also quite fast with a free movement. The Auxois is notable for its kind, quiet temperament and willing nature, making it easy to train. Most tend to be bay or roan, but some are chestnut – all without white markings. The bloodline includes Boulonnais and Percheron, but since the early 1900s the only other breed allowed to develop the Auxois has been the Ardennais. Never bred in very great numbers, the Auxois is still not common but is now used in the northwest of France around the Loire and the Côte d'Or for forestry, in the vineyards and in the tourist industry to pull horse-drawn caravans. It is also sometimes specifically bred for milk or meat.

BOULONNAIS

Although not officially recognized until the 17th century, the Boulonnais is an ancient breed possibly descended from the heavy horses of the pre-Christian era bred to Numidian horses brought by the invading armies of Julius Caesar. After the Crusades and the Spanish occupation, oriental and Andalusian blood was introduced – which gives the Boulonnais its refinement and elegant build. The breed is often considered to be the finest heavy horse and is used to improve the bloodline of other breeds. It is noted for its free-flowing action, stamina and endurance, as it is able to maintain a good speed over long distances. Once it was famous for pulling fish carts from the coast to Paris to deliver the fresh catch, and was often used as a carriage horse. Today its use is limited and numbers are low, although the French government funds a programme to save it from extinction.

COUNTRY: France
BLOOD TEMPERATURE: Cold
HEIGHT: Up to 17 hands
COLOUR: Usually grey, can be black, chestnut
ENVIRONMENT: Cool temperate
USES: Heavy draught
TEMPERAMENT: Lively but amiable
DESCRIPTION: Fine head with expressive eyes, gently curved neck, sloping shoulder, broad chest, strong legs with light feathering, bushy tail

BRETON

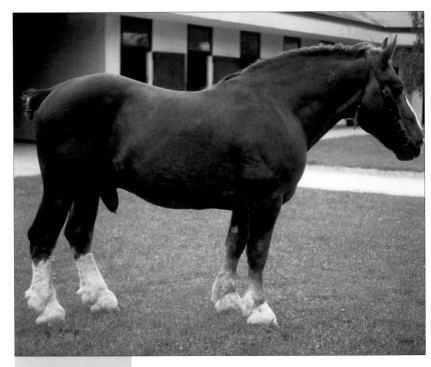

COUNTRY: France
BLOOD TEMPERATURE: Cold
HEIGHT: 15–16.3 hands
COLOUR: Chestnut with flaxen mane and tail, roan
ENVIRONMENT: Temperate
USES: Heavy and light draught
TEMPERAMENT: Amiable, easy-going
DESCRIPTION: Large head with straight profile, short arched neck, compact body with broad muscled quarters, short strong legs with minimal feathering

Originating from Brittany, or Bretagne, in northwest France, the Breton may have descended from horses brought to the area by the warrior Celts, or by Aryans migrating from Asia. It resembles horses from the Russian steppes, but at the time of the Crusades oriental blood was added and later that of Ardennes, Percheron, Boulonnais and the Norfolk Roadster. There are three types of Breton, from different areas. The Heavy Draught is bred around the northern coast and is renowned for its great strength, the Corlay or Central Mountain Breton is the result of crosses to Arab and Thoroughbred and is closest to the ancient type, and the Postier Breton has Norfolk Trotter and Hackney blood and makes a good coach horse — it was once used as an artillery horse. The Breton is still used on small farms and to gather seaweed and is the most numerous heavy draught horse in France.

COMTOIS

The Comtois is an ancient breed that is believed to have existed in the Franche-Compté and Jura areas of France, on the border with Switzerland, since the 4th century. It was probably brought to the area by the Burgundians, who had migrated from northern Germany; in the 16th century it was used to improve the horses of Burgundy. The Comtois was valued as a cavalry and artillery horse, used by the armies of both Louis XIV and Napoleon. In the 19th century it was crossed with the Norman Cob, Boulonnais and the Percheron and later with the Ardennes, which improved its strength. The Comtois is known for its endurance, hardiness and balance and is still used to haul wood in the mountains and to work in hilly vineyards of the Arbois; it is the second most numerous draught horse in France, after the Breton.

COUNTRY: France
BLOOD TEMPERATURE: Cold
HEIGHT: 14–15.1 hands
COLOUR: All shades of chestnut with flaxen mane and tail
ENVIRONMENT: Temperate
USES: Draught
TEMPERAMENT: Easy-going and willing
DESCRIPTION: Large head with a straight profile, short muscular neck, broad deep chest, rounded body, powerful quarters, strong legs with minimal feathering

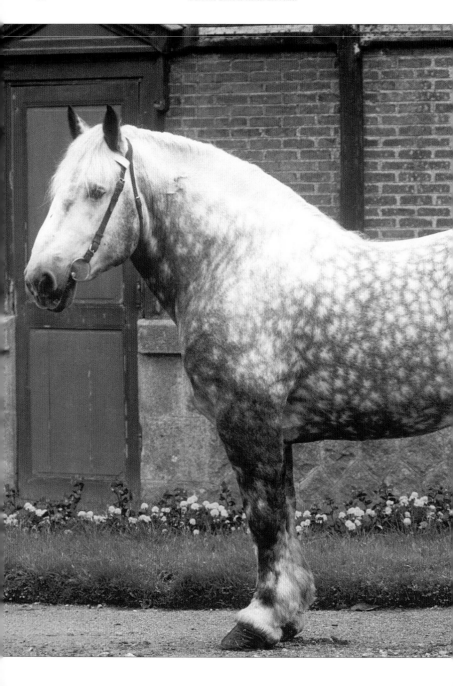

PERCHERON

The exact history of the Percheron is not clear, but one theory is that they are descended from Arab horses abandoned by the Moors in the 8th century in the region of La Perche in northern France, which were bred to Flemish stock. At the time of the Crusades the Percheron was already valued as a beautiful and stylish warhorse, even-tempered and very hardy. In the 17th century, traditionally the Percheron was used to pull the heavy mail coaches across France and the breed was also in demand as a farm horse. Later the French government imported two Arab stallions to breed with the Percheron, aiming to develop a mount for the army, and the most famous Percheron stallion, Jean le Blanc, was subsequently foaled in 1823. The breed is now used for carriage work in cities and for draught on small farms and also often appears in driving competitions at shows.

COUNTRY: France
BLOOD TEMPERATURE: Cold
HEIGHT: 14.3–16.1 hands, can be up to 17.2 hands
COLOUR: Grey, black
ENVIRONMENT: Cool temperate
USES: Draught, harness, riding
TEMPERAMENT: Even tempered
DESCRIPTION: Fine head on a long neck, deep broad chest, short strong back, muscled quarters, short muscular legs with little feathering

A Concise Guide to Horses and Ponies

NORMANDY COB

COUNTRY: France
BLOOD TEMPERATURE: Warm
HEIGHT: 15.3–16.3 hands
COLOUR: Chestnut, bay
ENVIRONMENT: Cool temperate
USES: Light draught, harness
TEMPERAMENT: Easy-going, gentle but lively
DESCRIPTION: Plain head on a short muscular neck, good shoulders, wide deep chest, short compact back, sturdy legs

Although Normandy in the northwest of France has been renowned as horse-breeding country since the 10th century, the Normandy Cob has only been around since the 19th century. It was first developed to meet the needs of the military, mainly at the state stud at Saint-Lô in the La Manche region but also at the nearby Le Pin stud. The breed developed along two lines – the lighter version also had Thoroughbred and Norfolk Roadster blood, and was used as a riding horse; the stockier and heavier light draught type was used for farm work. Traditionally the tail of the draught type was docked, but today may be plaited and bound instead. The draught type is most common today and is still used for agricultural work, mainly in the La Manche area. Although the breed is well established, there is no official stud book.

POITEVIN

The Poitevin, also sometimes known as the Mulassier, is not well known outside its native France. It originates from the Poitou region in the southwest of the country and is thought to be descended from heavy horses brought from Norway, Denmark and the Netherlands in the 17th century to drain the marshes and swamps. Although powerful, the Poitevin is lethargic and rather unattractive, so is little used as a work horse. However, when crossed with the local Baudet de Poitou donkey, it produces the most excellent Mule, which is particularly large and strong and was once highly valued all over Europe. After the Second World War the demand for Mules was greatly reduced and the Poitevin faced extinction, but recently a revival in interest in the Mule as a working animal has meant a corresponding interest in saving the Poitevin.

COUNTRY: France
BLOOD TEMPERATURE: Cold
HEIGHT: 16–16.3 hands
COLOUR: Dun, grey, bay, black
ENVIRONMENT: Temperate
USES: Draught, mule breeding
TEMPERAMENT: Generally good natured
DESCRIPTION: Heavy coarse head on a short muscular neck, straight shoulders, long straight back, short legs with very thick feathering

RHINELAND HEAVY DRAUGHT

The Rhineland Heavy Draught is sometimes called the German Coldblood or the Niedersachen Heavy Draught and was once found across the whole of Germany. It was developed in the second half of the 19th century, using mainly Belgian Draught and Ardennes as the foundation stock, with some blood from the British Clydesdale and the French Percheron and Boulonnais. The Rhineland Heavy Draught was an attractive animal, quite powerful and efficient, and was very popular for both farm work and for heavy draught – at one time it was the most numerous work horse found in Germany. However, after the Second World War numbers began to fall drastically as heavy draught horses were no long required and the breed is now quite rare and no longer has an official stud book. Instead, breeders have concentrated on developing a warmblood version, the Rhinelander.

COUNTRY: Germany
BLOOD TEMPERATURE: Cold
HEIGHT: 16–17 hands
COLOUR: Chestnut, roan, bay
ENVIRONMENT: Cool temperate
USES: Heavy draught
TEMPERAMENT: Easy-going
DESCRIPTION: Small well-shaped head, powerful arched neck, massive shoulders and quarters, short wide back, short legs with some feathering

SCHLESWIG HEAVY DRAUGHT

COUNTRY: Germany
BLOOD TEMPERATURE: Cold
HEIGHT: Up to 16.2 hands
COLOUR: Chestnut with
    flaxen mane and tail
ENVIRONMENT: Cool
    temperate
USES: Draught
TEMPERAMENT: Amiable
    and easy-going
DESCRIPTION: Attractive
    head on a short
    muscular neck,
    powerful shoulders,
    broad deep chest, long
    body, rounded quarters,
    short legs with heavy
    feathering

Originating from the north of Germany, the Schleswig
Heavy Draught takes its name from the Schleswig-
Holstein region. In the late 19th century the breed was
developed by the newly formed Schleswiger Horse
Breeders' Society, using Jutland and later Suffolk Punch
stallions. Most Schleswig Heavy Draught can trace their
ancestry through to a Suffolk Punch stallion called
Munkedal – son of Oppenheim LXII, who was imported
in 1860 to improve the Jutland breed. At the beginning of
the 20th century the Schleswig Heavy Draught was used
for farm work, to haul timber and as an artillery horse by
the military. Numbers fell after the Second World War,
and in the 1960s the breed was placed on the endangered
list. In 1991 the original breeders' association was
disbanded and the Society of Schleswiger Horse Breeders
was formed, which is dedicated to preserving the breed.

DUTCH HEAVY DRAUGHT

One of the newer breeds, the Dutch Heavy Draught was developed in Holland after the First World War, using Dutch mares bred to the Brabant, possibly with some input from the Belgian Ardennais. It is a massive and powerfully built horse with considerable strength, which means it can pull very heavy loads for long periods without tiring. Although generally quite slow moving and unhurried, it can move surprisingly fast when required. Despite its great size, it has a gentle temperament and is willing – and quite economical to keep. The soil in the area of its origin is heavy marine clay, which defeated many lesser breeds, but the Dutch Heavy Draught could cope with it easily. It was used mainly for agricultural work with some heavy draught and was once very popular, but like many other heavy draught breeds is now increasingly rare.

COUNTRY: Holland
BLOOD TEMPERATURE: Cold
HEIGHT: 16.2–16.3 hands
COLOUR: Chestnut, bay grey, sometimes black
ENVIRONMENT: Cool temperate
USES: Draught, agriculture
TEMPERAMENT: Willing, amiable
DESCRIPTION: Medium head with straight profile, short neck, heavily muscled shoulders and quarters, wide strong back, sturdy legs

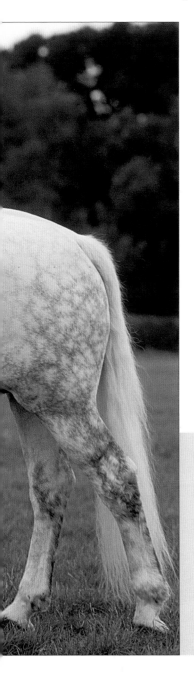

IRISH DRAUGHT

The Irish Draught is a true all-rounder, once used for all kinds of work on the farm, in harness on the family carriage and also for riding and hunting across country. It is descended from indigenous Irish horses crossed with the Great Horse brought by William the Conqueror, but later with Andalusian blood added so is lighter than most traditional draught breeds. The Irish Draught is energetic and graceful and is often crossed with the Thoroughbred to create the Irish hunter – which is one of the world's best mounts for cross-country riding – while its hard feet mean it is also ideal for breeding show jumpers. Although at the end of the 19th century – the time of the Irish Famine – numbers were considerably reduced, the Irish Draught is currently found in good numbers with breed societies in Britain, the United States, Canada, Australia and New Zealand

COUNTRY: Ireland
BLOOD TEMPERATURE: Warm
HEIGHT: 15.2–17 hands
COLOUR: All solid colours
ENVIRONMENT: Cool temperate
USES: Riding, hunting, light draught
TEMPERAMENT: Easy-going and docile
DESCRIPTION: Attractive head on a well-set neck, powerful shoulders, muscular body and quarters, good legs with no feathering

NORTH SWEDISH HORSE

COUNTRY: Sweden
BLOOD TEMPERATURE: Cold
HEIGHT: 15–15.2 hands
COLOUR: All solid, but often chestnut, brown or dun
ENVIRONMENT: Taiga
USES: Light draught, harness, forestry
TEMPERAMENT: Even tempered and willing
DESCRIPTION: Heavy pony-type head, short crested neck, long body with strong back, sloping shoulders, short strong legs with some feathering

The stud book for the North Swedish Horse was only established in 1909, but the breed is descended from the ancient Forest Horse. Over the years the blood of Friesian, Oldenburg and other European heavy horse breeds was added to the bloodline – and that of the Døle Gudbrandsdal, a specialist harness racer from Norway, which has similar ancestry. After the stud book was established, breeding was more strictly controlled to preserve the characteristics of the North Swedish Horse, which is known for its good temperament, longevity, courage and great strength for its size. The breed is ideally suited to the harsh Swedish winters and is resistant to most equine diseases. Although its numbers declined with the onset of mechanization it is still used in forestry work, while a lighter trotter line is the only coldblooded harness racer in the world.

ITALIAN HEAVY DRAUGHT

Developed in northern Italy in the 19–20th centuries, the Italian Heavy Draught was once the most numerous horse in Italy. Italian horses were initially crossed with the Brabant, Percheron and Boulonnais in an attempt to improve the local stock, but it was not until Breton stallions were added to the mix that a suitable breed was developed. Mostly the conformation is now good, although the breed does have a tendency to poor legs with small joints and boxy feet, which are both undesirable features. However, the Italian Heavy Draught is also attractive, energetic and fast moving – in Italy it is often called the Tiro Pesante Rapido, which means Fast Heavy Draught. Although numbers are now much lower than they were in the breed's heyday, it is still used in Italy on small farms – although it is also specifically bred for meat.

COUNTRY: Italy
BLOOD TEMPERATURE: Cold
HEIGHT: 15–16 hands
COLOUR: Mainly chestnut often with flaxen mane and tail, can be bay or roan
ENVIRONMENT: Temperate
USES: Draught, meat
TEMPERAMENT: Usually good natured
DESCRIPTION: Good head on an arched neck, powerful shoulders, compact muscular body with a strong back, short legs often with small feet and some feathering

TYPES

HUNTER

Although the hunter may vary in appearance, it has some common characteristics; it should be well balanced, fast, good at jumping and with lots of courage to face the unexpected. It is generally accepted that the best hunters are a mix of Irish Draught, for substance and common sense, mixed with Thoroughbred, for strength, speed and courage. Other breeds can also be involved, such as the Cleveland Bay, which can impart good jumping ability. The exact mix can depend on where the hunter is to be used – flat grassy areas, where speed is important, would require a higher percentage of Thoroughbred blood. The criteria also include stamina, since the hunt can go on all day and enthusiasts may go out several times a week. Hunting as a sport began in Britain in the 15th century, but in 2005 traditional hunting with hounds was banned in England and Wales – although it is still popular in parts of Europe and in North America.

COUNTRY: Britain
BLOOD TEMPERATURE: Warm
HEIGHT: 16–17 hands
COLOUR: All colours
ENVIRONMENT: Temperate
USES: Riding
TEMPERAMENT: Generally good
DESCRIPTION: Varies, but should have attractive head, long neck, good shoulders, broad deep chest, compact body, muscular legs

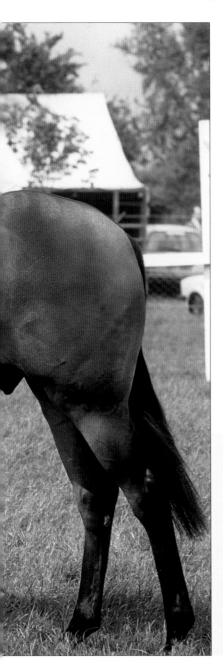

HACK

The hack is an elegant show horse, which not only has to look good but to have a graceful action in the show ring and be supremely well mannered. A peculiarly British phenomenon, in the 19th century there were two different types. The covert hack, which was ridden to the hunt but not used for hunting, had to look good and have a smooth pace but was not required to have much stamina – the closest equivalent today is the riding horse. The park hack was ridden by fashionable socialites in places where they wanted to be seen, like Rotten Row in London's Hyde Park. The park hack had to have real presence, good paces and excellent manners, since its main function was to show the rider to best advantage – today's equivalent is the show hack. Most show hacks are either Thoroughbreds or Anglo-Arab cross – although too much Arab blood is not desirable.

COUNTRY: Britain
BLOOD TEMPERATURE: Warm, hot
HEIGHT: 14–15.3 hands
COLOUR: All solid colours
ENVIRONMENT: Temperate
USES: Riding
TEMPERAMENT: Well-mannered with a calm disposition
DESCRIPTION: Quality head with a straight profile, elegant neck, nicely sloping shoulders, well-proportioned back, rounded quarters, legs long below the knee

RIDING PONY

Although it is essentially a scaled-down equivalent of the show hack, the riding pony should still retain some pony characteristics. It was first developed in Britain to perform in show riding classes and was based on native breeds such as the Welsh Mountain, Welsh Pony or Dartmoor usually crossed with a small Thoroughbred or sometimes an Arab. One particular Arab that sired a very successful line of riding ponies was the stallion Naseel. Ideally the resulting riding pony should be graceful and refined, with the long, low freedom of movement of the Thoroughbred. The riding pony has only been developed since the beginning of the 20th century, and since it is based on several breeds it has a range of coat colours – although not piebald and skewbald. It has become popular all over the world and is now bred in several different countries, including France, Germany, America and Australia.

COUNTRY: Britain
BLOOD TEMPERATURE: Warm
HEIGHT: 12–14.2 hands
COLOUR: All solid colours
ENVIRONMENT: Temperate
USES: Riding
TEMPERAMENT: Easy-going and polite
DESCRIPTION: Well-proportioned pony-type head, deep girth, compact body with well-muscled quarters, well-formed legs

COB

Although there are two breeds of cob – the Welsh and the Normandy – there is also a cob type, which does not have the same fixed breeding pattern. A true all-round horse, it can either be used under harness or ridden – it is strong enough to carry a full-grown man all day, but calm enough for children to ride. Show horses must walk, trot, canter and gallop in the ring and the mane is often trimmed right back – or hogged – to show off the jaunty line of the neck. In breeding, the cob may be either a pure Irish Draught, or this breed crossed with the Welsh Cob or Thoroughbred, or even with the Cleveland Bay. Usually thick set and powerful, they are designed to carry weight rather than for speed – although they can still go surprisingly fast when they get under way.

Country: Britain
Blood temperature: Warm
Height: 15–15.3 hands
Colour: All colours, including piebald and skewbald
Environment: Temperate
Uses: Riding, harness
Temperament: Well-behaved
Description: Attractive head on a short arched neck, broad deep chest, solid compact body, muscular rounded quarters, well-formed but short legs

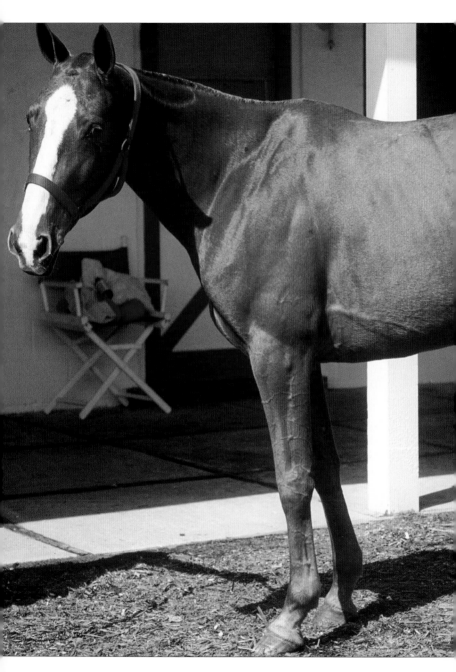

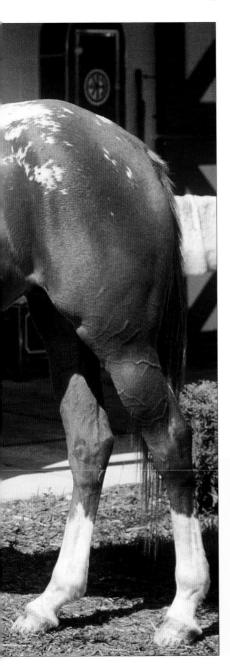

POLO PONY

Despite its name, the polo pony is not a pony. As a type, it was developed specifically for the game of polo – which requires speed, stamina, courage, good balance and great agility, as well as an animal that is responsive, turning quickly on demand. Like the cob's, the polo pony's mane is usually trimmed back, or hogged, so it does not become entangled in the polo stick during the game. The game of polo possibly originated in Persia in 525 BC, but the British became interested in the game in India in the 19th century and introduced it to Europe and the Americas. Initially most polo ponies were bred in Britain, but they are now more likely to come from Argentina. They are usually based on the Thoroughbred, often bred to the Criollo and increasingly with Quarter Horse blood, since this breed has a reputation for being particularly responsive.

COUNTRY: Argentina
BLOOD TEMPERATURE: Warm, hot
HEIGHT: Average around 15 hands
COLOUR: All colours, including piebald and skewbald
ENVIRONMENT: Temperate grassland
USES: Riding
TEMPERAMENT: Intelligent and courageous
DESCRIPTION: Attractive head on a lean muscular neck, lean wiry body, muscular quarters, tough straight legs, hard feet

MULE

The mule is a cross between a female horse and a male donkey – a female donkey and a male horse give a hinny, although they are both often covered under the general term of mule. Using different horse breeds results in different sizes and weights – the mule can be anything from a miniature 90 cm (36 in) up to 17 hands. Exceptionally strong with excellent stamina and usually a quiet temperament, the mule has been celebrated as a working animal. Its reputation for being stubborn is in reality the manifestation of intelligence – a mule knows when enough is enough and will refuse to do any more! Both mules and hinnies are usually sterile, so a constant supply of horses and donkeys is required to produce more. The most celebrated breed of horse when it comes to mule production is the Poitevin, or Mullasier, which gives particularly fine, large, hardworking mules.

COUNTRY: Most, but particularly North America
BLOOD TEMPERATURE: N/A
HEIGHT: Can be up to 17 hands
COLOUR: All colours, but not true pinto
ENVIRONMENT: All
USES: Draught, harness, riding
TEMPERAMENT: Patient, intelligent
DESCRIPTION: Varies, usually a donkey-type head with quite long ears, upright mane, sturdy body, long tail

GLOSSARY

above the bit – when the horse carries its head high, so that the level of its mouth is above the level of the rider's hand, reducing the rider's control.

action – how the horse's frame moves in the act of locomotion.

aged –a horse that is 7 years or older.

aid – a signal given to the horse by the rider or driver, communicating what the horse is required to do. Aids include movements of the legs, hands and body weight, or voice instructions (natural aids) and the whip or spur (artificial aids).

airs above the ground – exercises of the *haute école*, or classical equitation, in which either both forelegs or all four feet leave the ground.

back at the knee – a conformational fault in which the forelegs are curved back below the knee.

backed – the process of mounting and riding a young horse for the first time, as in 'this horse is ready to be backed'

barrel – the horse's body from behind the shoulder to the loins

bars of the mouth – the area of the mouth in the lower jaw between the incisors and the molars, where the bit rests.

behind the bit – when the horse holds its head with the chin brought in close to the chest to evade the rider's control.

blood stock – Thoroughbred horses bred specifically for racing.

bone – a measurement of the horse's bone taken just below the knee or the hock; the larger the circumference of the bone, the more weight-carrying ability the horse should have.

bosomy – an over-heavy chest.

bow-hocked – a conformational defect in which, when looking at the horse from behind, the hocks appear to be bowing out from each other. See also cow-hocked.

boxy feet – hooves that are excessively narrow and upright in formation, with a small frog and closed heel, like those of a donkey.

breaking – the early schooling or training of a horse.

breed – a group of horses that has been bred for specific characteristics over time, with the details of pedigree recorded in a stud book.

broad and deep – with reference to the chest; a well-structured, wide chest. Traditionally, a bowler hat was placed between the two front legs directly under the chest to indicate a good size.

brood mare – a mare kept specifically for breeding.

brushing – a faulty action in which the horse strikes the fetlock and lower leg region with the hoof or the shoe of the opposite foot.

buck – a horse leaping into the air with its back arched and coming down with lowered head and stiff forelegs.

buck-knee – see back at the knee.

bung tail – see docked.

calf-knee – see back at the knee.

cannon bone – shin bone of the foreleg between the knee and the fetlock.

capped elbows – when a swelling occurs in the elbow area as a result of a direct blow or chafing. This can also happen at the hocks, in which case it is called capped hocks.

carriage horse – a light horse bred specifically for pulling a carriage.

cart horse – a heavy horse bred specifically for pulling a cart.

capillary test – pressing the gum with a thumb to temporarily restrict the flow of blood to this area. When the thumb is removed the blood should immediately flow back into the capillaries. If this takes longer than normal it is a sign of ill health.

charger – a horse bred specifically as a mount for military officers.

clean-legged – a horse with no feathering on the lower part of the leg.

coach horse – a powerful horse bred specifically for pulling a coach.

cobby type – a horse with a conformation similar to a cob – stocky, sturdy and strong, with short legs and a rounded barrel.

coldblood – generic name for heavy horses, mostly European breeds descended from the now extinct Forest Horse.

colt – an uncastrated male horse that is under four years old.

coloured – see part-coloured.

concussion – the jarring caused to the horse's foot and lower leg by the impact of the foot hitting the ground.

condition – the general state of health of a horse.

conformation – the way the horse is constructed, particularly in reference to the proportion of each body part to each other.

cover – the mating between a mare and a stallion.

cowboy – someone who makes a living working on a ranch with cows.

cow-hocked – a conformational defect in which, when looking at the horse from behind, the hocks appear to be turning into each other. See also bow-hocked.

cow-sense – a particular aptitude for working cows; a horse with cow-sense is able to anticipate the cow's next move.

crib-bite – a habit of chewing on stable door, fences or any hard surface. This is an undesirable habit that can develop into windsucking.

cross-breed –mating two horses of different breeds.

daisy-cutting – a low walking or trotting action, particularly in Thoroughbreds and Arabs.

dam – the female parent of a horse.

dappled – coat colouring with a pattern of darker hair, often in a circular or semi-circular pattern, overlaying a lighter coat.

dorsal stripe – a dark stripe running from the withers along the spine to the top of the tail, most commonly seen on dun coat colouring. Occasionally seen in conjunction with wither stripes.

dipped back – see sway back.

dished face – a concave profile.

dishing – a faulty action in which the front legs from the knee down are thrown outwards in a circular motion.

docked tail – amputation of the tail for aesthetic reasons.

engaged hocks – a good action, with the hind legs well underneath the horse and not trailing out behind the quarters.

ergot – the small horny growth at the back of the fetlock joint.

ewe-necked – a conformational defect in which the neck has an over-developed muscle underneath and a concave outline above.

extravagant action – moving with knees and hocks lifted high at each step, as seen in the Hackney breed.

farrier – a person trained and qualified to shoe and trim a horse's feet.

feathering – long hair on the lower part of the legs, most often abundant on heavier horse breeds and some highland ponies.

feral – an animal that was once domesticated but has been released or escaped into the wild and has become established there.

filly – a female horse generally under four years old.

flea-bitten – grey coat colouring with a quantity of black hairs distributed throughout, giving a freckled appearance.

flexion – when the horse yields to the bit through the jaw, with the head bent in the correct position through the poll with no tension or resistance.

foal – a colt, gelding or filly that is not yet 12 months old.

forearm – the top part of the horse's front legs, above the knee.

forehand – the horse's forelegs, shoulders, neck and head, from the withers forward.

forelock – the section of mane coming forward over the forehead between the ears.

four-square – a horse that is solidly built and appears to have 'a leg at each corner'.

frog – the wedge-shape elastic horny pad on the sole of the foot, which helps grip and absorb shock.

gaited horse – an American term for a horse that has either natural or trained gaits.

gelding – a male horse that has been castrated and is therefore unable to reproduce.

girth – a body circumference measurement taken behind the withers; a good depth of girth is a desirable conformational feature indicating plenty of room for lung expansion.

going – a neck that is well-proportioned to the body and set well on a good shoulder.

good length of rein – a neck that is well-proportioned to the body and set well on a good shoulder.

good front – a horse with a long sloping shoulder and a good neck length that carries its saddle set back.

hack – a type of light horse for riding; to go riding.

half-bred – the progeny of two different breeds of horse.

hand – a unit of measure in relation to a horse's height, dating back to medieval times. One hand is equal to 10 cm (4 in.); a horse is measured in hands and inches, so 15.2 hands would be 15 hands and 2 inches high.

harem – a band of mares presided over by a stallion in the wild.

harness – the equipment for a horse being driven – not used for that of a riding horse.

harness horse – a powerful horse bred specifically for use in harness, with straighter shoulders.

haute école – literally means 'high school'; the art of classical equitation; advanced dressage movements.

heavy horse – a heavier horse, with a powerful body and good stamina but limited speed, usually used for draught work.

high set tail – a tail springing from high on the quarters; the horse tends to carry the tail high, which can be eye-catching.

hindquarters – See quarters.

hollow back – see sway back.

hogged – horse that has had its mane shaved or clipped off, commonly seen in polo ponies and cobs. Also known as a roached mane.

hot blood – a term used for Arabs, Barbs and Thoroughbred breeds.

inbreeding – breeding a horse to a close relative to accentuate particular characteristics.

in-hand – a horse that is not being ridden; in shows paraded on a halter.

in heat / in season – a mare who is in her oestrus cycle and likely to be receptive to a stallion.

jibbah – the shield-shaped bulge on the forehead of an Arab horse

kicking boards – wooden boards placed around the inside wall of a stable up to a height of 1.2 m (4 ft). Also sometimes around the inside walls of an indoor or outside school, but usually to a lower level.

kicking boots – felt boots placed on the back feet of a mare before she is covered by a stallion, to protect the stallion if she kicks him.

knock-kneed – knees that appear to bow toward each other.

koumiss – drink made from fermented mare's milk.

leg at each corner –used to describe a horse with a good deep chest and ample room between the airs of legs.

light-boned – a conformational fault in which the measurement of the bone below the knee is too small in comparison to the size of the horse. Sometimes referred to as light of bone.

light horse – a riding horse other than a pony or heavy horse.

line breeding – mating horses of different generations but with a common ancestor, to accentuate specific characteristics.

loaded shoulder – excessive muscle development over the shoulder, which inhibits movement.

loins – area of the back on either side of the spine, behind the saddle and in front of the quarters.

low-set tail – tail springing from low on the quarters, which can be a sign of weak and sloping quarters.

mare – fully-grown female horse.

mitbah – the arched angle at which the Arabian horse's head meets its neck; it allows particular all round freedom of movement.

nap/nappy – used to describe a horse that refuses to go forward as directed; usually exhibited when the animal is being asked to leave the company of other horses.

nicked – having had the muscles under the tail divided and reset to produce an exaggerated high tail carriage.

numnah – protective pad worn beneath the saddle.

on the bit – horse carrying its head near vertically with the mouth just below the rider's hand.

Oriental horse – a general term for any breed of horse originating from the East.

outcross – breeding to an unrelated horse, or introducing blood from outside the breed.

overbent – see behind the bit.

overreach – a horse striking into the heel of the front foot with the toe of the hind foot.

pace – a trotting gait with the legs moving in lateral pairs, rather than the conventional diagonal pairs.

pack horse – horse or pony used to transport goods on its back, usually in a pack saddle specially designed for the purpose.

part-coloured – skewbald or piebald horse.

pedigree – the details of an animal's ancestry, usually recorded in a stud book.

piebald – coat colour with patches of black and white.

pigeon-toed – a conformational defect in which the horse's toes turn inward.

pinto – the American term for a part-coloured horse.

plenty of bone – used to describe a horse with a generous circumference at the bone below the knee; generally 20 cm (8 in.) or more.

poll – top of the head between the ears.

primitive – having features of primitive horse breeds, such as dun colouring, dorsal stripe and heavy head.

pulling the mane – thinning and shortening the mane by removing hairs from the underside to improve its appearance. Can also be done to the tail.

quality – indicates a horse with evident good breeding and refinement; quality usually comes from having either Arab or Thoroughbred blood.

quarters – the area of the body from the flank backwards to the start of the tail.

racehorse – horse specifically bred for racing, most often used to describe a Thoroughbred.

recoil test – pinching the skin of the neck; on release the skin should recoil immediately. If it does not it indicates the horse is unwell or suffering from dehydration.

roach back – convex curving of the spine; opposite of dipped back.

roached mane – see hogged.

school – ride a horse to train for a specific purpose.

sclera – the white outer membrane of the eye, seen often in the Appaloosa.

sickle-hocked – a conformational fault in which the horse has weak hocks, with the joint angled too steeply, which results in weak hindlegs.

sire – the male parent of a horse.

skep – plastic or rubber container, similar to a basket, used to collect droppings in the stable.

skewbald – coat colour with patches of white and another colour, usually brown.

slab-sided – a horse with a flat ribcage.

soft condition – a horse that is healthy but not fully fit and lacks muscle development.

stallion – uncastrated male horse over four years old.

stud book – book kept by a breed society, recording the pedigree of each horse eligible for entry.

stud – breeding establishment.

sway back – back that dips excessively in the middle, most often seen in older animals; opposite of roach back.

tack – popular name for saddlery items.

teaser – stallion used to test if a mare is in season and will be receptive to mating.

thin soles – when the area of the underneath of the foot is susceptible to bruising easily.

tied-in below the knee – a conformational fault in which the horse has a smaller measurement of bone below the knee than above the fetlock.

toad eye – eye with a heavy top lid, as on the Exmoor pony.

top-line – line of the neck from the withers to the poll. A good top-line will have a gently upward curve.

type – horse that fits into a function group, such as hunter or hack, but is not a specific breed.

turned away – period of rest after a young horse has been backed. Also used to describe a horse turned out to grass for a holiday.

warmblood – generally horses that are crosses of Thoroughbreds or Arabs with other bloods.

weaving – when a horse stands and rocks from side to side, an undesirable vice that can strain the front limbs.

well let-down – with reference to the hocks; hocks close to the ground with the first and second thigh well muscled.

well-set – swith reference to the neck or head; good conformation, with the junction between head and neck correctly placed.

well-sprung – with reference to the ribs; nicely rounded ribcage, allowing plenty of room for heart and lungs.

windsucking – an undesirable vice in which the horse grips a solid object with its teeth, tenses its neck muscles and swallows air down. In severe cases the horse does this without fastening onto anything, which can result in indigestion problems.

wither stripes – dark line extending out from the withers on either side, down towards the shoulders. Usually seen in conjunction with a dorsal stripe.

INDEX

PICTURE CREDITS

All images in this book are courtesy of Kit Houghton
Photography except those listed below

Bob Langrish: 94, 106, 109, 120, 124, 171, 207 and 224

Thank you to Kit and Kate Houghton, Debbie Cook and Bob
Langrish for all their help in the production of this book.